Islams and Modernities

PHRONESIS

A new series from Verso edited by Ernesto Laclau and Chantal Mouffe

There is today wide agreement that the left-wing project is in crisis. New antagonisms have emerged – not only in advanced capitalist societies but also in the Eastern bloc and in the Third World – that require the reformulation of the socialist ideal in terms of an extension and deepening of democracy. However, serious disagreements exist as to the theoretical strategy needed to carry out such a task. There are those for whom the current critique of rationalism and universalism puts into jeopardy the very basis of the democratic project. Others argue that the critique of essentialism – a point of convergence of the most important trends in contemporary theory: post-structuralism, philosophy of language after the later Wittgenstein, post-Heideggerian hermeneutics – is the necessary condition for understanding the widening of the field of social struggles characteristic of the present stage of democratic politics. *Phronesis* clearly locates itself among the latter. Our objective is to establish a dialogue between these theoretical developments and left-wing politics. We believe that an anti-essentialist theoretical stand is the sine qua non of a new vision for the left conceived in terms of a radical and plural democracy.

Islams and Modernities

AZIZ AL-AZMEH

VERSO
London · New York

First published by Verso 1993

Verso
UK: 6 Meard Street, London W1V 3HR
USA: 29 West 35th Street, New York, NY 10001-2291

Verso is the imprint of New Left Books

ISBN 0-86091-451-8
ISBN 0-86091-626-X (pbk)

British Library Cataloguing in Publication Data
A catalogue record for this book is available from the British Library

Library of Congress Cataloging-in-Publication Data
A catalogue record for this book is available from the Library of Congress

Typeset in Scantext September by Solidus (Bristol) Limited
Printed in Great Britain by Biddles Ltd, Guildford and King's Lynn

Contents

Acknowledgements

The Prologue was delivered at the conference on L'Islam en Europe – L'Islam vue d'Europe, held in Aix-en-Provence in November 1992.

Chapter 1 is an edited amalgam of two texts: "Universalism, Democracy, Islam and the Arabs" was presented to a conference at the Collège International de Philosophie in Paris; "Islam as a Political Category" was prepared for the 15th World Congress of the International Political Science Association in Buenos Aires, July 1991. I am particularly grateful for comments from Jean Leca, Richard Rorty, Olivier Mongin and from exciting audiences.

Chapter 2 was originally a paper delivered to the East–West Philosophers' Conference, Honolulu, in 1989. It was published in Eliot Deutsch, ed., *Culture and Modernity*, University of Hawaii Press 1991. Copyright permission is gratefully acknowledged.

Chapter 3 was published in *Review of Middle East Studies*, 4, 1988.

Chapter 4 was delivered at a conference on cultural transitions in the Middle East, The American University, Washington, in 1989. It was published in the *History Workshop Journal*, 32, 1991. Copyright permission is gratefully acknowledged.

Chapter 5 is the text of a public lecture delivered at the Free University, Berlin, 1988. It was published in *History of Political Thought*, XI, 1990. Copyright permission is gratefully acknowledged.

Chapter 6 was published in Ian R. Netton, ed., *Arabia and the Gulf*, London, Routledge, 1988. Copyright permission is gratefully acknowledged.

Chapter 7 was delivered as an Inaugural Lecture at the University of Exeter. It was published as a pamphlet by the Department of Arabic and Islamic Studies, University of Exeter.

قال ابن المقفَّع : إياكَ والتتبُّعَ لوحشيٍّ الكلام طَمَعاً
في نَيْل البلاغة

Beware of pursuing savage speech in
your quest for eloquence.

Ibn al-Muqaffaʿ
(d. 759)

PROLOGUE

Muslim "Culture" and the European Tribe

> Un Parisien est tout surpris quand on lui dit que les Hottentots font couper à leurs enfants mâles un testicule. Les Hottentots sont peut-être surpris que les Parisiens en gardent les deux.
>
> Voltaire

The essays assembled in this book derive from the contention that there are as many Islams as there are situations that sustain it. European Islam in its various forms and places is no exception. It is perhaps a measure of the potency of the imaginary Islam as it is conceived in mediatic representation and according to the spontaneous philosophy of "experts", academics included, that this elementary contention needs to be defended at a time like ours. We can surely assume that among the permanent acquisitions of the social and human sciences is the realization that ideological and other forms of collective representation are unthinkable without internal change and structural bearing. And it is a fact that this acquisition is almost invariably put to use in the study of contemporary ideologies, mass movements and other phenomena of European histories and realities. But it is not generally put to use regarding *phenomena islamica*, which are regarded as generically closed, utterly exotic, repellently mysterious, utterly exceptionalist.

I do not wish to elaborate much on this pervasive and unflinching misrecognition, although I suggest, in this and in subsequent essays, many factors that make it prevalent. For now, I am commenting on the recent transition, most specifically in Britain, from structural considerations of immigration to a culturalist notion of ethnic diversity which has come to predominate in the past two decades and which was consecrated by the Rushdie affair. There are definite structural foundations for this transition in the popular consciousness, and there is little mystery in this that cannot be unravelled with reference to elementary notions of ideology, in which relations of subordination and domination are sublimated,[1] so that a fetishism of "culture" becomes a part of the social imaginary of advanced capitalism and its new divisions of labour on the international scale. Thus and in the first instance, primary importance must be attributed to the impossibility of socio-economic assimilation experienced by second-generation immigrants born in situations of urban degradation and into marginal, declining and unskilled industry, at a time of increasing state indifference and hostility coupled with racism in the very capillaries of the "host society".[2] Added to this are pressures that push Asian Muslin (and other) shopkeepers to cater for the poorest, as slum landlords and purveyors of cheap goods, and thus take on the classic features of a middleman minority confronted with racist reactions.[3] The work of the ethnic entrepreneur, operating through kinship networks which provide the basis for domestic commodity production as well as for the sweatshop, is a classic condition conducive to social involution,[4] and the formation of social as well as geographical ghettos. Finally, modern communications have enhanced the sense of immigrant deracination by facilitating the illusion of truth to the realities of the country of origin, a sense reinforced by the reality, made possible by increasing globalization, of transnational economic and social networks which forms a central part of immigrant life.

Thus structural and spatial segregation and social involution and ghetto formation lie at the basis of the culturalism that is now becoming the prevalent mode of discourse as the non-European presence in Europe, most particularly of Muslims who, for a host of reasons not connected with historical or social reality, are assumed to form a community by virtue of sharing a religion which, peculiarly, has been dubbed a "culture". The reader will note that concrete material adduced in support of my arguments here concerns exclusively British Muslims of Pakistani origin, and it is indeed with them that the following paragraphs are chiefly concerned. Like other groups, British Muslims of Pakistani origin constitute a specific configuration of socio-economic locations. Yet generalizations about social groups in terms of religion in order to describe their specificities and to underpin factors that overdetermine their socio-economic and ideological positions have become habitual, although they are irresponsible, for the forces that make for social involution are not religious;[5] religious difference underwrites and does not overdetermine social exclusivism. The hyper-Islamization of collectivities of Muslim origin has accompanied hardening tendencies to social involution premised on structural features of communities of Muslim origin. This representation, which assumes a homogeneity overriding differences between those of rural and of urban origin, rich and poor, educated and illiterate, is by no means a reflection of social reality, which is one of stunning diversity.

Some Britons of Pakistani origin, like the Kashmiris of Mirpuri origin, who predominate in Bradford, are of rural origin with hardly any social awareness of city life even in Pakistan itself. Their culture is above all rural, with Muslim religious elements incorporated within this primary determination – but Muslim religious elements of a mystical and magical character, unconnected to the legalism of the puritanical Islam of their advocates and spokesmen. Their rural origin explains that tendency to be far more socially conservative on matters such as girls' education than Indian Muslims, for instance, who belong to a different "culture" born of different geographical, social and educational imperatives.[6] Facts such as the reasonable integration of wealthier Pakistanis within their class in Britain, the regional conditions of origin and socio-economic diversities among the Pakistanis of Britain (not to speak of British Muslims generally – certainly not a corporate group)[7] – are often overlooked. Also habitually ignored are the facts of class division among Pakistanis, with the religious authorities leading the representation of the poorer sections as far back as the late 1970s,[8] and the fact that there were forces for integration as well as for involution among British citizens of Pakistani origin before the Rushdie affair, including generous openness to knowledge, no matter how reserved, of Christianity and of the ambient society.[9] In the same vein of mystification, the considerable alienation of young Pakistanis, especially girls, from their background is ignored.[10] Instead, emphasis is exclusively laid on the undeniable forces for involution and ghettoization. Features observable and ascendant since 1989 are projected back into an indistinct, though very proximate past.

Of these features one might cite many indices. Some are connected with kinship networks,[11] which, among Pakistanis as others, are increasingly international and encourage life in a fantasy of rootedness. Others are newer. An interview with a marriage bureau owner who serves the British Pakistani community indicates a growing tendency for men in Britain to seek wives from Pakistan rather than from British-bred Pakistani women, and of the former they are choosing increasingly younger and more cloistered girls of more conservative outlook.[12] Other features are the proliferation of exclusivist Muslim organizations, like Young Muslims' annual fairs, Muslim fun-fairs, Muslim medical advisory services, not to speak of an unelected Muslim parliament. With the Rushdie affair, a number of Muslim internationalist infrastructures of an educational, welfare and propaganda nature (beholden to networks controlled by Iran, Saudi Arabia and the Pakistani *jamaat-i islam-i*) were put into high gear and conjured up the notion of an "Islamic community" as a distinctive and identifiable entity. But it must not be assumed that these and cognate phenomena are in any sort of continuity, direct or indirect, with the Muslim "culture" of origin, for there is no such culture at origin, and the trans-Islamism we witness is highly recherché, and specific to the present and the very recent past, as well as to Britain and to political interests articulated here in the name of Islam.

Thus the presumptions of Muslim cultural homogeneity and continuity do not correspond to social reality. Muslim reality in Britain is, rather, composed of many realities, some structural, some organizational and institutional, but which are overall highly fragmentary.[13] Nevertheless, abstracted from its socio-economic bearings, European Islam, and Islam *tout court*, has been represented as a cohesive, homogeneous and invariant force, indeed an otherness so radical that it is possible to speak of it as a historical enemy, much in the same way as communism was addressed in some circles.[14] It is represented as a repellent exoticism by mass psychological mechanisms very like those involved in anti-Semitism.[15] Yet the median discourse on Islam in Britain as in Europe is not predominantly or always overtly racist or quasi-racist. What we have is a culturalist differentialism; we are presented with supposed differences of "culture" within a discourse which can be either heterophiliac or heterophobic:[16] both are premised on irreducible and impermeable difference.

Now culture, like nature, is one of the most difficult notions to use in the social sciences. This difficulty is compounded by the fact that its increasingly pervasive and irresponsible use has come to indicate little beyond an aesthetic of otherness, and more generally a negative aesthetic of otherness, which invigilates ideological processes that oversee the constitution of specific identities under specific conditions of socio-economic confinement, buttressed by what is known, in the "host" society, as multiculturalism.

The origins of this exclusivist and differentialist notion of culture are quite straightforward. A culturalist relativism *avant la lettre* was available in the repertory of European social thought from the time of Romanticism in the late eighteenth and early nineteenth centuries and was counterposed to the universalist notions of civilization – "Politically, as so often in this period, it veered between radicalism and reaction and very often, in the confusion of major social change, fused elements of both".[17] Thus differentialist culturalism comprehends both a libertarian streak and a segregationism, today as well as in its places of origin, as mirror images, with anti-racist heterophilia mirroring racist heterophobia, or indeed like racist heterophilia which wants "cultures" to coexist in mere spatiality without interpenetrating. The trajectory of this notion of "culture", in the nineteenth century, was one in the course of which it was elaborated as racism along biologistic lines,[18] and the irrationalist vitalism of this notion is still its most active constituent. In the course of the past two decades, three displacements affected this notion: race became ethnicity, then culture; normative hierarchy and inequality gave way to representation in terms of difference; and heterophobia was in many circles replaced by heterophilia.[19] Thus we find fused in racist and anti-racist discourse alike the concept of non-transmissible life-styles, a concept garnered by the race relations industry, the Labour Party and professional ethnology deriving from the heritage of the German Romantic historical school and from British functionalist anthropology alike.[20]

It is irrelevant to the force of this differentialist culturalism that it is tied to a specific vantage point in both time and place. This is a cosmopolite, post-imperial (but not necessarily post-imperialist) North with a particular grid of misrecognition to which is commonly applied the cliché "postmodernism".[21] This is a fictitious sense of novelty and of radical diversity primed to become automatically operational as a means of ideological and representational uniformization whenever collective representations of global and local social and political conflict are called forth.[22] It is a shibboleth which reduces realities to Reality, expressed in bytes, and therefore amenable to manipulation; in other words, a recent form of the ideological production which had previously been termed "the end of ideology".

Culturalist differentialism is born equally in a situation of a radical notion of ascriptive individualism, a social condition which is projected on to a metaphysical screen describing universal conditions. And finally, in Britain, this condition is equally engendered by a tradition, become a knee-jerk policy of husbanding internal and external affairs, of politico-ethnic and politico-cultural categorization which, in the past, resulted in the catastrophic divisions of India, Palestine and Ireland, and which today results in regarding as natural – therefore not worth the effort of resistance – both the ghettoization of Britain and "ethnic cleansing" in the Balkans.

This culturalist differentialism nevertheless, and despite the individualistic liberalism of its proponents, exists in "a vicious circle of complicity" with heterophobic racism.[23] It has in Britain completely internalized the Powellite notions about nations or other collectivities being predetermined boundaries of sympathy, overdetermined by an instinctivism[24] which does not need to present itself necessarily in terms of racial hatred: all it requires is a "discursive deracialization" underpinned by exclusivism and "arguments from genuine fears" premised on the supposed authority of "common sense".[25]

Like racism, culturalist differentialism is an essentialist perceptive system premised on a notion of a pregiven "culture" which, like race, has no sociological definition. Culture is here an obscure term coined to schematize without precision an indeterminate reality.[26] Indeed, it is the enormous advantage of this notion that it is put forward to indicate sheer difference, for in this sense it can not be disproved because it is tautological: chicken tandoori is not roast chicken; a black headscarf is not a fashion accessory; Muslim prayer is not a High Church Christmas mass.[27] In all, tokens of a banal nature are taken up and affirmed as tokens – or stigmata – of difference, and differences elevated to Difference based in an absolutization of heritage which, although cultural, is attributed to a state of nature in which cultures subsist, according to this discourse.[28]

In the chapters that follow the reader will find ample elements of a discourse on "cultures" of an Islamic name that contextualizes them into the flow of historical and social forces, and thus deculturalizes and demystifies them. What remains to be done here is symptomatically and briefly to examine some aspects of another actor in this "vicious circle of complicity", namely, the British Muslim advocates of culturalist Islamism.

There is no doubt that British Muslims, most particularly those of Pakistani and, to a somewhat lesser extent, of Bengali origin, are witnessing a heightened sense of religiosity, albeit against a background of Bengali adherence to secular nationalist rather than to religious political advocacy.[29] Until recently, religiosity was connected with upward social mobility among the poorest elements, and correlated to intra-communal competition.[30] The Rushdie affair accelerated this tendency and made public a number of sentiments and stigmata which have become part of public mythology and hence have taken on autonomous trajectories[31] in the construction of inter-communalist myths, and thus in the generation of putative identities. Initially disembodied from social practice, religious vision and ritual observance under conditions of migration to Europe takes on a certain autonomy from social processes and prescribes an autonomist notion of the religious ego and a body of allied prescriptions.[32] It also proffers a fetishism of the collective self as a socio-political imperative.

Thus Islamic "culture" takes on the aspect of a psychodrama, and the serious business of inventing a culture begins, primarily by the conjuration and proclamation of tokens (stigmata to others) of exoticism, particularly ones which give a pronounced visual edge to the boundaries of exclusion/inclusion. Basic and most plastic among these are dressing up, and exhibitionistic piety, with dramaturgical direction provided by such political or quasi-political organizations as are poised to take over this new political constituency, with the full complicity of the heterophiliac/heterophobic "host culture", the one in the name of "multiculturalism", the other with an apartheitic intent closer in spirit to the advocates of this exclusivism themselves. A past is invented, sensibilities discovered. It therefore becomes possible to assert, for instance, that Rushdie's use of the now infamous "Mahound" is provocative,[33] although there is no tradition of awareness of this name in either medieval or modern Islam, and knowledge of this name was, until 1989, the preserve of a handful of Western antiquarians, who might well and justifiably object that it is far more complex than opponents of Rushdie imagine. Yet "Mahound" is given the status of "popular" knowledge quite artificially. Suddenly, we hear of "an authentically Islamic temper" and of what constitutes a "real Muslim".[34] We hear of "cultural treason" against Muslims[35] and opponents of this phantasmagoric trend, like the present author, are dismissed as "Christian" because they dispute the conjurations of the Islamist party. We also encounter positions of sanctimonious sentimentalism as "Muslim sensibility" without further qualification, and are told of arcadian scenes of spring cleaning in Damascus by "Muslim housewives",[36] although Christian Damascene households are by no means less fastidious about cleanliness – and indeed Damascene Muslim micro-sociological lore, to which I can testify at first hand, regards Christian housewives as rather more fastidious than Muslims, and their houses and streets somewhat neater. An ethnographic account tells of women in Pakistani households supervising children reading in the back room – reading the Koran only is mentioned, not homework.[37] It also tells of Mughal families taking pride in their descent from Muslim conquerors, with too much accent on religion and too little on nobility[38] – the properly Muslim nobility consists of *sayyids*, not Mughals, whose title to nobility is conquest and statehood. Thus blanks in personal sanctimoniousness or naïve research are filled with fanciful material weighted towards misrecognizing reality as a constituent in the Islamist psychodrama. And the primary victim, Salman Rushdie himself, edging towards compromise at a particular moment, recast his intellectual genealogy in such a way that the Arabian Nights, the influence of which he professes, became "Islamic" literature.[39]

A sentimentalist view of a spurious, unsullied reality prior to the corruption of the present, or of such a fantastic reality continuing in the present, is then made into the main constituent of a political and social programme, as subsequent chapters of this book will indicate in some detail. This spurious prior reality is termed "culture". It is neither "real" nor old, but is a recherché cluster of modes of visible behaviour which are said by certain Islamist authorities to represent the "true prior reality' – one that British Pakistani Muslims had never known until recently, for it is not only traditions that are invented, but also collective memories. The most notable title under which this politics of nostalgia for an imagined past is officiated is of course the "application" of Islamic law: a law which was never a code that could be "applied', as the Appendix to this chapter indicates. This "law" is supposed to distinguish a *genre de vie* which is as impermeable as it is intransitive, and therefore deserving of the title "culture". It is thus that the politics of nostalgia imagines a past, or a prior reality, conjures an affection for a past that never was, and turns this sentimentalist imperative into a programme to be imposed on the social and political realities of today.

All in all, therefore, we have, in the play of this psychodrama, an efflorescence of fantastic genealogies and explanations, all premised on heterophobic/heterophiliac differentialism, from the flirtations of the willing Beauty and the eager Beast (such as the contributions of John Berger and David Caute to the Rushdie affair), through to the shrill xenophobia of a Fay Weldon or Anthony Burgess, across to the platitudinous liberalism of the median discourse of differentialism.

But there is more than psychodrama, self-parody and caricature in this explosion of the fantasy. For we have the steady accumulation of pressure points on the education system (with a view to creating Muslim schools where girls could be properly socialized) and elsewhere with a view to detaching British Muslims, especially Asians and most particularly Pakistanis, from the mainstream of modern life, and their resocialization within a new culture of exclusivism and xenophobia. This is the impact of the calls for Muslim communalist institutions,[40] with a subculture in the process of invention. Such, for instance, is the case of the Yummies (young, upwardly mobile Muslims), who stand against non-liberal liberalism, who dress sharply in clothes to pray and play in, who cloister together in home-centred communities, immune from the vices of the ambient society, but nevertheless sharing housework.[41]

But British Muslims are perhaps no more than a case in point in the Europe of the Lombard League, of Jean-Marie Le Pen, of minuscule regionalism. Muslim differentialist discourse, a counter-racism or a racism in reverse, would seem appropriate in a Britain where culturalist differentialism has, as mentioned, fully internalized the Powellite conception of history as the savage play of ascriptive sympathies and antipathies, in which the "natural" condition of groups of different origins is one in which they are wholly apart, and in which any attempt to mix them would render conflict inevitable. Such is perhaps natural in a Europe that regards itself as tribal territory with precise border controls, in which nations (for some sections of their members) regard themselves as tribes, all ranged above one another according to a tributary model of subalternity. Such, in an age of dubious postmodernity, is the consequence of "the new Cartesianism of the irrational".[42] And such is the natural outcome of a situation in Croatia and Serbia succinctly described by an outstanding columnist, a situation which is not alien to Western Europe except in sheer density and extent – but intensity is by definition shifting and conjunctural, and it is not clear to what extent the West European body politic is systemically immune to this:

> Miraculous Virgins make their scheduled appearance. Lurid posters show shafts of light touching the pommels of mysterious swords, or blazoning the talons of absurd but vicious two-headed eagles. More than a million Serbs attend a frenzied rally, on the battle site of Kosovo, where their forebears were humiliated *in 1389*, and hear former Communists rave in accents of wounded tribalism. Ancient insignias, totems, feudal coats of arms, talismans, oaths, rituals, icons and regalia jostle to take the field. A society long sunk in political stagnation, but nevertheless across the threshold of modernity, is convulsed: puking up great rancid chunks of undigested barbarism.[43]

Tribalism, heterophila, heterophobia and Islamist exclusivism alike are premised on a very classical trope of modern European irrationalist political and social thought (hence its attractiveness to postmodernism) – right-wing Romanticism,[44] with the attendant organicism of its notions of history, the corporatism of its notion of society, and the voluntarism of its notion of political action. These matters will be discussed in Chapter 1.

Appendix: Blasphemy and the Character of Islamic Law

When in 1608, King James asked the jurist and parliamentarian Sir Edward Coke why it was that law could not be interpreted by any intelligent man in the light of reason, Sir Edward resorted to an argument for the technical nature of legal reason:

> True it is that God has endowed Your Majesty with excellent science, and great endowments of nature; but Your Majesty is not learned in the law of this your realm of England, and causes which concern the life, or inheritance, or goods, of fortune of your subjects, are not to be decided by natural reason, but by the artificial reason and judgement of the law,

> which law is an art which requires long study and experience before that a man can attain to the cognizance of it.

A response of the same nature could be given by any jurist with technical competence in the field of Islamic law to the claims made for this law by advocates of Islamist political ideologies. These advocates claim to speak for a univocal body of legislation which is not grounded in the vast historical experience of Muslims. They also speak in terms of explicit and demonstrable commands deriving from scriptural statements without the mediation of legal reason. Finally, they give the impression, and sometimes make the utopian presumption, of a universal extraterritoriality which has no grounds in Islamic scriptures or in the historical experience of Muslims.

This may not be surprising. This advocacy is made by ideologues with at best a rudimentary knowledge of Muslim scriptures. In the case of divines with undisputed knowledge of Islamic scripture and legal texts, it arises from the suspension of such knowledge in favour of immediate ideological and political purposes. It is unfortunate that an impression of ferocious crudity and simplicity is being given of Islamic law, an impression which is certainly undeserved by the vast corpus of writings on law and legal methodology (deontic logic, analogical connections, rhetorical methods, philological and lexical procedures) stretching over centuries and vast expanses of territory, the ensemble of which is Islamic law.

The first characteristic feature of Islamic law which ought to be indicated as a corrective concerns its technical nature. Islamic law is highly technical, indeed arcane, to those who have not sought properly to tackle its vast body of literature. Some of the great jurists such as Sarakhsī, the greatest figure in the Hanafite school to which the vast majority of Indian Subcontinent Muslims adhere (along with Afghans, Turks and the Arabs of Syria and Iraq) went to great lengths to demonstrate that his notions and procedures are so technical that they have none but a most tangential connection with ethical or dogmatic considerations.[45] The divine origin of some of the utterances which enter the conveyor belt of legal reason – that is, the text of the Koran – is technically irrelevant to their legal aspect. Infractions of law are punishable in this world, infractions of divine purpose in the next. This must be the first matter to bear in mind today, when ignorance and politics are wilfully confusing Islamic law with the requirements of Islamist ideology.

The second point concerns legal innovation. Contrary to political and ideological pretensions, the historical reality of the practice of Islamic law has been one of wide latitude in opinions over specific points of law (the *ikhtilāf*). The corollary of this, quite naturally, is the mutability of this law in the context of changing circumstances, a mutability which does not accord with the utopian archaism of Islamist politics. And indeed, the reform of Islamic law over the past century has instituted a condition of "absolute discretion" (*ijtihād muṭlaq*) based on the reinterpretation of scriptural and other foundation texts, in addition to what Islamic legal theory designates as the "auxiliary" sources of law: custom, public interest and equity. The prevalent trend in Muslim law reform in the present century has indeed been an attempt to generalize the classical precepts in such a manner as to have them merge with a notion of natural law; such has been the achievement of the great reformer Muhammad Abduh. In theoretical terms, Muslim jurists (though not the Shiʿa) have adopted a highly sceptical view of the finality of their judgements; hence the readiness mutually to recognize views that may be contradictory. It is recognized – though this recognition is not shared by Islamist ideologues – that it is against natural justice and natural law (which accords with divine will) to foist ordinances of relevance to the seventh century upon the twentieth.

Moreover, Islamic law is not a code. This is why the frequently heard call for its "application" is meaningless, most particularly when calls are made for the application of *sharīʿa* – this last term does not designate law, but is a general term designating good order, much like *nomos* or *dharma*. Islamic law is a repertoire of precedents, cases and general principles, along with a body of well-developed hermeneutical and paralogical techniques. In certain respects, it resembles English law quite strongly; one can study these connections (as with Germanic law) in the seminal work of the Arab world's premier jurist of this century, A. Sanhury,[46] and of his French associates, Edouard Lambert, Linant de Bellefonds and others. This characteristic nature of Islamic law reinforces its legal latitudinarianism, a fact which explains how it emerged and reigned successfully as one of the great legal systems of the world over more than twelve centuries in very different parts of the globe. Little wonder, then, that Islamic law has a predominantly objectivist character, as Sanhury and his associates have shown. This (in marked contrast to French law) reinforces its technical nature and further accentuates its being the preserve of fully trained jurists.

One final point must be mentioned. Islamic law as a corpus is predominantly private: it treats of obligation, contract, personal status (including succession) and other aspects of secular life. These are termed by Islamic jurists *ḥuqūq al-ʿibād*, the rights of persons. A much smaller corpus of public law exists under the rubric *ḥuqūq Allāh*, the rights of God. These concern the obligations incumbent upon properly constituted Islamic polities; they are redundant in the absence of such a polity and have no extraterritorial competence, and a Muslim *in partibus infidelium* is a *mustaʾmin* "under safe conduct", obliged to follow the laws of his or her country of residence. Substantively, the rights of God concern protecting and maintaining the Muslim body politic through international relations both martial and pacific, and through invigilating its internal integrity by the creation of a *Rechtsstaat* and the suppression of ideological sedition – that is, unbelief, apostasy and the very difficult notion of blasphemy.

Apostasy as a legal notion was questioned in the Middle Ages, abolished in Ottoman territories before the middle of the nineteenth century, and regarded by the famous Muslim reformer of the present century, Muhammad Rashid Rida, as a political matter concerning the seventh century and, as such, of no consequence to the present age; indeed, the Koran states quite unequivocally that there should be no compulsion in matters of religion (*la ikrāha fid-dīn*). Unbelief and blasphemy have had different meanings and accents over the historical experience of Muslims, although there does exist a hard core of dogmas which are universally held, regardless of their historical justification; all traditions harden in this manner. Additionally, all traditions vary, over time and place, in the severity and in the systematic character with which unbelief and dogmatic deviance are pursued. Likewise, most traditions reach a point where doctrinal purity and univocality become redundant. Such is the case with those parts of the world with Muslim majorities, especially in the Arab world, except for subcultural pockets and among political minorities which espouse a fundamentalist primitivism entirely inattentive to the historical experience of Muslims and to the historical character of their law. Islam has, moreover, never had a central authority which determines rectitude and which has exclusive title to the legitimacy which renders its territories the Abode of Islam, and thus the location of the practice of the Islamic legal system. This is especially so in modern times, when the Rights of Persons have been partly incorporated into the civil codes of such countries as Egypt, Syria and Iraq (all the achievements of Sanhury), but according to modern legal principles. What was not thus incorporated has been forgotten – and even such as was codified has lost its "Islamic" and taken on an entirely civil character. The Rights of God, on the other hand, though rarely abolished in any explicit manner, have been left in abeyance and relegated for exaction in the next world.

Thus any consideration of the question of blasphemy or of heresy, be it that of Mr Rushdie or of others, must first face the historical irrelevance of his task, and must also be cognizant of its technical impossibility in the very terms of the Islamic legal corpus and system themselves. Calls for the "application of Islamic law" have no connection with the Muslim legal tradition built upon multivocality, technical competence and the existence of an executive political authority which controls the legal system. It is a political slogan, not a return to a past reality.

Notes

1. Veronique de Rudder, "L'Obstacle culturel: la différence et la distance", *L'Homme et la société*, January 1986, pp. 39, 45.

2. See, among many others, ibid., p. 29; Verity Saifullah Khan, "The Pakistanis: Mirpuri Villagers at Home and in Bradford", in James L. Watson, ed., *Between Two Cultures: Migrants and Minorities in Britain*, Oxford 1977, pp. 75–6, 80, 86 and passim; Tariq Modood, "British Asian Muslims and the Rushdie affair", *The Political Quarterly*, 6/1–2, 1990, pp. 145 and passim.

3. Pnina Werbner, "Shattered Bridges: The Dialectics of Progress and Alienation among British Muslims", *New Community*, 17, 1991, pp. 342–3.

4. Haleh Afshar, "Gender Roles and the 'Moral Economy of Kin' among Pakistani Women in West Yorkshire", *New Community*, 15, 1989, pp. 211–26.

5. Saifullah Khan, "The Pakistanis", pp. 58, 74, 80, 86.

6. Daniele Joly, "The Opinions of Mirpuri Parents in Saltley, Birmingham, about their Children's Schooling", Centre for the Study of Islam and Christian–Muslim Relations, Birmingham, *Research Papers – Muslims in Europe, no.* 23, September 1984, pp. 20–21.

7. For instance, Werbner, "Shattered Bridges", pp. 342–3.

8. Pnina Werbner, "Ritual and Social Networks. A Study of Pakistani Immigrants in Manchester", unpublished PhD thesis, Manchester

University, 1979, pp. 338–9.

9. Werbner, "Shattered Bridges", pp. 339 and passim; Paul Bhai, "Image of Christian Life among Muslim Residents – A Study of Birmingham", unpublished dissertation for the Certificate in the Study of Islam, Centre for the Study of Islam and Muslim–Christian Relations, Birmingham, 1979, passim.

10. R. Sharif, "Interviews with Young Muslim Women of Pakistani Origin", Centre for the Study of Islam and Christian–Muslim Relations, Birmingham, *Research Papers – Muslims in Europe, no. 27*, 1985, pp. 11, 14 and passim.

11. Saifullah Khan, "The Pakistanis", pp. 58, 74 and passim.

12. *Muslim News*, 23 March 1990; Modood, "British Asian Muslims", p. 147.

13. Modood, "British Asian Muslims", passim; Jørgen Nielsen, "A Muslim Agenda for Britain: Some Reflections", *New Community*, 17, 1991, especially p. 472.

14. An example of this vulgar discourse is Daniel Pipes, *The Rushdie Affair. The Novel, the Ayatollah, and the West*, New York 1990, pp. 214 ff.; and see Aziz Al-Azmeh, "The Middle East and Islam: A Ventriloqual Terrorism", in *Third World Affairs, 1988*, London 1988, pp. 23ff.

15. T. Adorno in Theodor Adorno et al., *The Authoritarian Personality*, New York 1950, ch. XIX.

16. On differentialism, heterophilia and heterophobia, see in general Pierre-André Taguieff, *La Force du préjugé. Essai sur le racisme et ses doubles*, Paris 1987.

17. Raymond Williams, *Keywords*, London 1976, s.v. "Culture".

18. Colette Guillaumin, *L'Idéologie raciste. Genèse et langage actuelle*, Paris and The Hague 1972, ch. 1.

19. Taguieff, *La Force du préjugé*, p. 14.

20. Claude Lévi-Strauss, *A View from Afar*, transl. J. Neugroschel and P. Hoss, Harmondsworth 1987, p. 26.

21. On this phenomenon, the reader is referred to Alex Callinicos, *Against Postmodernism*, Cambridge 1989; David Harvey, *The Condition of Postmodernity*, Oxford 1989; and Fredric Jameson, *Postmodernism, or, the Cultural Logic of Late Capitalism*, London 1991. Highly pertinent here is a reminder of Herbert Marcuse, *One Dimensional Man*, London 1964.

22. See Christopher Norris, *Uncritical Theory. Postmodernism, Intellectuals, and the Gulf War*, London 1992.

23. Taguieff, *La Force du préjugé*, pp. 16, 43, 416.

24. Martin Barker, *The New Racism: Conservatives and the Ideology of the Tribe*, London 1981, pp. 14 ff., 97, and chs 3 and 4 passim.

25. Frank Reeves, *British Racial Discourse: A Study of British Political Discourse about Race and Race-Related Matters*, Cambridge 1983.

26. Guillaumin, *L'Idéologie raciste*, pp. 2, 13; Taguieff, *La Force du préjugé*, pp. 19ff.

27. Cf. de Rudder, "L'Obstacle culturel", pp. 32–3.

28. Cf. Taguieff, *La Force du préjugé*, pp. 15–16; Etienne Balibar in E. Balibar and E. Wallerstein, *Race, Nation, Class: Ambiguous Identities*, London 1991, pp. 17–18, 21–2, 57.

29. See especially, Stephen William Barton, *The Bengali Muslims of Bradford*, Leeds 1986, pp. 184–5.

30. Werbner, "Ritual and Social Networks", pp. xxv, 60ff, 357.

31. Werbner, "Shattered Bridges", pp. 344–5.

32. Werner Schiffauer, "Migration and Religiousness', in T. Gerholm and Y.G. Lithman, eds, *The New Islamic Presence in Western Europe*, London and New York 1988, pp. 151–2, 155.

33. Malise Ruthven, *The Satanic Affair*, London 1990, p. 36.

34. For instance Shabbir Akhtar, *Be Careful with Muhammad*, London 1989, p. 7 and passim.

35. Ali Mazrui, in L. Appignanesi and S. Maitland, eds, *The Rushdie File*, London 1989, pp. 221–2.

36. Rana Kabbani, *Letter to Christendom*, London 1989, pp. ix, 19–20, 35, 37 and passim.

37. Alison Shaw, *A Pakistani Community in Britain*, Oxford 1988, p. 64.

38. Ibid., p. 93.

39. Interview in *The Guardian*, 17 January 1991.

40. See particularly the sweet reasonableness of Modood, "British Asian Muslims", passim.

41. *Muslim Wise*, January 1990, pp. 14–15.

42. Umberto Eco, *Travels in Hyperreality*, transl. W. Weaver, London 1987, p. 129.

43. Christopher Hitchens, "Appointment in Sarajevo", *The Nation*, 14 September 1992, p. 236.

44. Romanticism was a central feature of Western political discourse in the past 200 years, but is very little recognized and imperfectly known, and is usually and quite erroneously regarded as marginal in studies of Western political thought. See the recent overview of Michael Löwy and Robert Sayre, *Révolte et méloncholie. Le romantisme à contre-courant de la modernité*, Paris 1992, chs 1 and 2. The authors of this rather traditional history of ideas are, without justification, keen to save Romanticism from fascism and the religious right, which they classify as "reactionary modernism" (pp. 93ff, 237). This gloss is contrary to interpretations made in this book, particularly in the next chapter.

Tzvetan Todorov's *On Human Diversity: Nationalism, Racism, and Exoticism in French Thought* (transl. C. Porter, Cambridge, MA, 1993) alas only came to my attention after this book had gone to press. But I should like to signal the meticulous detail with which Todorov treats the possible transformations of essentialist relativism (chs 2 and 3 passim, especially pp. 219ff) and the ease with which racism can give way to culturalism (pp. 156–7).

45. See Baber Johansen, "Die Sündige, gesunde Amme. Moral und

gesetzliche Bestimmung (hukm) im islamischen Recht", *Die Welt des Islams*, 28, 1988, pp. 264–82.

46. See Enid Hill, "Islamic Law as a Source for the Development of a Comparative Jurisprudence: Theory and Practice in the Life and Work of Sanhuri", in A. Al-Azmeh, ed., *Islamic Law: Social and Historical Contexts*, London 1988 pp. 146–97; and Aziz Al-Azmeh, *Al-ʿIlmānīya* [Secularism], Beirut 1992, pp. 211ff.

1

Islamism and the Arabs

There is a growing tendency to reduce the politics of the Arab World to the play of infra-historical forces. A simple glance at recent writing and mediatic representations of Iraqi politics following the capitulation of the Baghdad regime would reveal that the complex processes unfolding are glossed quite simply, and with the supreme confidence of ignorance, as a contestation between various transcendental essences: Shiʿism, Sunnism, Kurdism, with epiphanies of merely peripheral consequence: the Kurdish Democratic party, the Baath party, the Takriti clan, the Daʿwa party. Of even less consequence, and incomprehensible in terms of the above, are curious entities such as the Iraqi Communist Party (once the most powerful organized political force in the country). It is as if the social and political forces accountable in terms of history are elided to make way for *pneumata* simultaneously subjacent to history and superordinate to its flow.

Islamism and Neo-Orientalism

The spirits that animate what in this image is the repetitive flow of Arab history and politics are, in the literate and semi-literate patois of today, firm *identities*, specificities which in their turn animate a discourse of radical irreducibility which constructs the theory that Arab society and politics constitute a mosaic: a metaphor for congenital antagonism between infra-historical entities, most particularly religious, sectarian and ethnic affiliations. These are presented as pure facticities, bereft of conditions, as identities intrinsically and definitively constituted prior to and beyond acts of constitution and without conditions of constitution, as social essences which, without mediation, become political forces: such are Shiʿite insurrections, Sunni regimes, Kurdish rebellions, without further qualification. These selfsame spirits are the transhistorical essences to which all matters revert once history has, it is claimed, manifestly failed in subverting the continuity of these savage identities: history in its various ruses as nationalism, democracy and socialism. Thus it is claimed that universalist historical forces fail to make headway against the transhistorical *Volksgeist*, and are subject to almost immediate degeneration: nationalism to sheer religious xenophobia, democracy to corruption and manipulation, socialism to extortion and travesty. In other words, infra-historical forces, such as primary communal, religious or regional forms of social organization, are taken for the markers of suprahistorical continuity.

This metaphysical discourse on identity is not new. It was taken for granted in classical orientalist writing on the present condition of the Arab World, a discourse in which antiquarian erudition provided the material on which continuity and identity were established on bases which were ostensibly firm, and which proferred knowledge which enracinated the future, as well as the actually existing present – in contradistinction to the merely visible, in the Hegelian sense – in what it took to be its proper bearings, that is to say, in the past, in the vehicle of invariant *Geist*. What is new today, however, is threefold: that this discourse of identity is taking place in the context of what is referred to as postmodernism and of the neo-orientalism associated with its movement, that it is buttressed with a pseudo-sociological explanation, and that it seems congruent with a political discourse of identity to the participants in this infra-historical contestation. I will examine these in turn.

There are specific conjunctural conditions of possibility for the neo-orientalist discourse on the identity of the other – most notably, Islam, both within and outside Europe and North America. Not the least of these is the conjunction of the manifest failure of modernist notions of economic development in the major parts of the Third World (including the Arab World and other areas of Muslim majority). Nor is it possible to overemphasize the international reorganization of capitalist production under the regime of "flexible accumulation", including the ethnic stratification of labour internationally and within advanced capitalist countries, and its attendant socio-ethnic stratification and ghettoization.[1] Along with these developments came changes in the character of the metropolitan state, from the "national-social" one built on the Republican model to one which sustains a web of connections with society so diffuse as to become a "state institution of the market"; this shift resulted in a redefinition of the notion of ethnic minority in Europe in far more accentuated form.[2] With these developments went the rise of the new libertarian right, most notably in the United States and in France with a "new philosophy" in the mediatic and oracular mode, and the expansion of fundamentalism in the USA and of the racist right in Europe. The demise of communism dealt the *coup de grace* to the nineteenth century with its modernist utopias of unilineal evolution and historical inevitability, but gave a new lease of life to its nationalist debris, particularly in Eastern Europe. It also exacted from certain intellectuals a ponderous and sometimes vengeful settlement of accounts with many an "erstwhile philosophical consciousness". The limitless *tiers-mondisme* of yesterday was sublimated and restricted not only to a consciousness of limits and differences, but to nihilistic assertions of closure officiated under the titles of relativism and liberalism. Such is the intellectual lassitude with regard to matters Islamic, that for the historical commonality provided by evolutionism in its various versions was substituted a notion of irreducible divergence. For historical rationality was substituted a banal historical relativism; for modernist developmentalism (or revolutionism) was counterposed a postmodernism of the pre-modern.

Ultimately, it is a finalist understanding of *difference* which underpins the above, a notion of difference that yields utterly to the wholly inappropriate surveyor's metaphor of incommensurability, to a notion of relativism which is open both to benign and to malign interpretations. In the former interpretation of relativism, an ethical assertion of mutual legitimacy masquerades as a form of the understanding, and constitutes an apology for otherness which cannot be cognitively maintained except after the most perfunctory fashion.[3] In the latter, we have an antagonism which by denial severely limits an identity[4] to an otherness/inferiority which is at once ineluctable and impermeable. In both, we have the language of the self – the self being an identity constituted by utterance on the Other in a particular conjuncture – taking itself for the "metalanguage of a cultural typology"[5] whose terms are generically closed, thus yielding finalist notions of the West, Islam, and so on. The relations between these entities are relations of difference and intransitivity; their ensemble is sheer plurality, mere geographical contiguity and, ultimately, total war, the other face of the savage and chimerical notion of identity in the course of a history, our "actually existing" history, which levels identities and devours them voraciously. For modernity – and, indeed, modernism in its various fields – is not confined to Europe, but is a universal civilization which from mercantile beginnings came utterly to transform the economies, societies, polities and cultures of the world, and to reconstitute the non-European world in terms of actually existing historical breaks.

Contemplating sheer difference in the manner described above transforms particularity into a metaphysic of particularism, anchored in a wonderfully archaic Romantic notion of history confined to the history of others. In the 1980s this relegation of the non-European world to irreducible and therefore irredeemable particularism was officiated, with increasing frequency and clearly as a mark of bewilderment, under the title of "culture", which became little more than a token for incomprehension: each "culture" is represented as a monadic universe of solipsism and impermeability, consisting in its manifold instances of expressions of an essential self, with each of these instances being a metaphor for the primary classifier – the West, Islam. Thus we have the invention of traditions, such as "Islamic" dress, an "Islamic" way of life, "Islamic" positions on various political matters, simulacra all of them of the invariant essence of Islam, a name which is posited as the final explanatory principle.

The pseudo-sociology used to justify the above invention of particularity is no other than the theoretical elaboration of this mystification. One could refer here to works on Islamism which have won some acclaim[6] but which in my opinion are distinguished chiefly by banality. It transpires on scrutiny that this pseudo-sociology devolves to no more than the common epistemological correlate of all ideological formations, namely, to a protocol for reducing the *history* of the present to the *nature* of the invariant essence; indeed so unmediated is this movement, so scrupulous in its regard for invariant tropes, that one would be better guided by Vladimir Propp to the understanding of these works than take them in conjunction with Weber and others to illuminate Islamic and other manifestations of otherness. An ideology of particularist specificity guides the sociological imagination towards regarding quotidian banalities as epoch-making and marking the boundaries of a chimerical cultural ego to the inside of which there can be no entry.

The major fallacies on which this pseudo-sociology of the other is built are the notions of essential homogeneity, transhistorical continuity and closure. It takes place within the medium of variants of a discourse of "authenticity", in which societies chosen as the field of application of the totalizing category "Islam" – "Islamic societies" – are thought to constitute a *Lebenswelt* with an essential and closed homogeneity. This leads to the confinement of political forms "natural" to it to those in keeping with a putative Islamic essence. These forms are essentially, as mentioned at the beginning of this intervention, an expression of the Islamic – or Shiʿite, or Sunnite – nature of society, in which exclusivist notions of identity, rather than some ascriptive notion of citizenship, defines political participation. These political forms also relate to society in a crude form of representation, premised on correspondence, and therefore on authenticity. In other words, and after the fashion of classical orientalism, society, polity and culture correspond immediately,[7] for it is only thus that they can together partake of an essence, and revert to nature.

Not surprisingly, particularly given a milieu of lapsed Marxism, the appeal to "authenticity" commandeers Gramsci and presents itself as the reclamation of "civil society" which Islamism is supposed to represent: a civil society, however, not as a "Kingdom of Ends", nor as a moment of the superstructure (as in Gramsci) or of the structure (as in Marx), but as societal protoplasm teeming with ontological might. This is the precise genealogy – or, rather, aetiology – of the notion of a "return" to Islam in the Arab world and elsewhere, a notion thoughtlessly used by almost all authors on Islamism and the Arab world.[8] The theme of "return" has become a discursive *topos* which facilitates the elision of history, of society, and of polity, and is one which not only sustains this segregationist discourse in the West, but is also a prime instrument of the totalitarian Islamist political claim totally to represent society, as we shall see below.

There is one notion correlative to the trope of "return" which is particularly pertinent here: the claim that non-Islamist political forces are not of autochthonous provenance, and not in correspondence with this protoplasmic identity. Thus socialism, liberalism and Marxism are not only extraneous, but *ipso facto* temporary, surface irruptions, the work of minorities out of keeping with the atemporal rhythm of the essence. This underlies the pseudo-sociological apology for Islamism popular in certain circles in France,[9] which defines "civil society" as those sectors of the body social that have not benefited from the modern Arab state, and relegates to marginality other moments of the various Arab historical formations (highly transitional entities, all), including the state, the paramount agency of modern history in the Arab World as elsewhere. More empirically minded American studies adapt this rhetoric of authenticity. One author[10] maintains that, though internal differentiation indeed obtains in Arab societies and polities, the "massive, glacial, and pitiable presence" of the religiously excitable plebs dictates an upper limit for any departure from fanatical frenzy: out of the bounds of "civil society" are, therefore, Marxism, and liberalism. The future lies with "Islamic liberalism" to which "the Muslim bourgeoisie" is confined.

Islam as a Political Category

It goes without saying that the position just outlined is part of what has been called "cultural development aid", for under unpropitious conditions, such as the lingering social and economic crises besetting Arab lands – in keeping with their Southern identity – liberalism is seen as permitting a set of stable political arrangements which will "either prevail worldwide, or ... will have to be defended by nondiscursive action".[11] The echoes of Fukuyama and his milieu are by no means fortuitous; both belong to the same moment – the present situation of monopolarity in international relations. The Islamist proclivity and apology of recent years in the West is a form of political intervention on the side of Petro-Islamic order yearning for realization in the wake of the cold war, which was played locally (in the Arab World) by the discourse of Islamist authenticity projecting an enemy in "imported ideologies", initially socialism in all its varieties, and especially Nasserism, and today liberalism.

Islamist revanchism in the Arab World is not a "return" to a primitivist utopia, although this is the manner in which it presents itself. Like its counterpart in Western writing, it subsists in a discourse of authenticity whose primary epistemological instrument is the recognition and registration of difference, and where the sacralization of politics is regarded not as a disguise, but as an unveiling. This is why Kepel,[12] for instance, rejects any consideration of the Islamist form of political expression in terms of ideology: he regards Islamism as neither mystification nor occlusion, but as revelation. It is in this same spirit that Islamist political organizations have throughout eschewed party politics, for they have always assumed, half in earnest and half with disingenuity, that they are above parties, being the authentic centre of whatever body politic they desire to dominate. Such domination is invariably interpreted as a return by that body politic to its Truth, the restoration of its nature and its spirit, the reassertion of its very Being.

Islam appears as an eminently protean category. It appears indifferently, among other things, to name a history, indicate a religion, ghettoize a community, describe a "culture", explain a disagreeable exoticism and fully specify a political programme. I do not propose here to anatomize this category in the salient forms it acquires in the folds of the social imaginary in its various discursive loci, where it is constituted within a polarized system of binary classification in which "the West" is taken as a normative metalanguage from which are generated, by negation, the tokens that together constitute the properties of "Islam": fanaticism, irrationalist traditionism, atemporality, and their many metonyms, each betokened by common images, such as crowds, the veil, postures of prayer, and so forth.[13]

What I do propose to do in the following paragraphs is to bring back to history the category of Islam, and to unveil the universalist convergences yielded by the political discourse of Islamist exclusivism. The discourse of political Islamism shares many features with the category of Islam common in the social imaginary of "the West" that I have referred to, and it will be seen that this is due to the fact that the two categorical formulations share common theoretical and historical conditions of emergence.

Political Islamism revolves around the advocacy of a political order which makes possible what is known as "the application of the *sharīʿa*". An alternative formulation to this consists of inserting the advocacy of this political order – let us call it an Islamic state – in terms that lie at the interface between an eschatological solution in terms of a salvation history and the realization of a utopia. The *topos* where the order of perfection exists is one in frozen time, for it is none other than the order of rectitude that reigned at the time of the Prophet Muhammad and of his immediate successors (the Medinan Caliphate), the order described in a voluminous corpus of quasi-sacred narrative scripture called the *ḥadīth*. This utopian order is therefore a collection of paradigmatic single acts and pronouncements of impeccable rectitude and felicity, and it is the selfsame body of paradigmatic single acts that constitute and have constituted the mass of legal precedents upon which Islamic law is erected. Thus it must be clear that there can be no justification in speaking of the "application" of the *sharīʿa*, as it is not a code, nor is it codifiable; rather it is a body of narratives relating to precedents to which is ascribed a paradigmatic status, acts most of which, although single, are by no means singular, as they have parallels elsewhere, in other traditions, or even, like various manifestations of sageliness, to be found universally.[14]

The first point established is therefore that the discourse of Islamist politics seeks the erection of a political order which makes possible the integralist implementation of a legalistic utopia whose elements are, for analytical purposes, both arbitrary and single, not being subsumable under any general category. From this, it would follow that there is no order of concatenation that binds these elements, but that the sole title by means of which they are joined together is their appurtenance to a name, Islam. In other words, Islam transpires to intend a repertoire of examples lent paradigmatic – indeed, sacred – status by subsumption under the normative cover of the name which sacralizes them and lends them a moral inevitability, and which alone carries the full amplitude of normativity within a set of elements, normative all of them, whose normative status is derived entirely from their association with the sacralizing name. Islam is therefore self-reference effected by transference; each element to which this sacral property is transferred – the veil, various regulations concerning dietary taboos and inheritance, elements of monotheistic dogma, certain types of commercial transaction, prohibition of usury, and so on – is in itself neutral had it not been for a value transferred to it. By this token, each of these elements is a metonym for Islam and stands for it fully. This is what makes it possible for "Islamic" regimes to consider the establishment of an Islamic state definitive, when primitive punitive codes and the prohibition of usury, and a small number of other tokens of Islamicity are implemented. For it is this property of things Islamic – that they are only nominally so – that gives tokenism a very hard sense and, concomitantly, renders the indication of things as Islamic an act which is only possible by the agency that effects the indication and the intention. The retrievable repertoire is immense; only a limited number of elements is reclaimed to betoken Islamicity, and this selection is a political act.[15]

The connection between the manner in which populism and the Islamic repertoire is articulated is very close. Like populism, this repertoire can never in itself constitute "the articulating principle of a political discourse".[16] The signifiers of Islamism are not always "floating", but for the most part they are exhumed by deliberate search among medieval works. Yet it is asserted by Islamists that these elements, *volens nolens*, form a continuous patrimony which belongs to all, like the elements interpellated in populism, and the node of interpellation, the nominative "Islam", is made to indicate elements that are by no means "popular", but are in fact arcane elements that are associated with the nominative and thus made to partake of the generality of intention attributed to it. Such are, for instance, certain manners of dress, like the "Islamic" dress women are increasingly compelled to wear, the result of general textual indications and of pious Cairene dress designers in the 1960s. Elements from the past – manners of dress for instance – are made Islamic, and therefore "popular", although they bear no relation to the manner in which people, Muslims included, dressed. This is underwritten by the primitivist trope that is a concomitant of populism,[17] and which is essential to Islamism, as it is this primitivism which provides it with its utopia.

Though neither "popular" nor "floating" except in part, the elements of this primitivist utopia are assimilated to the normative nominative "Islam" and are thus represented as "popular". This is done on the assumption that that which is Islamic is perforce popular; that which is not in actuality popular is merely occluded, and its retrieval and reinsertion in the populist protocol is an act of rehabilitating nature which contingent history has left in abeyance.

This is the first point at which Islamist discourse in general is articulated with ideology and becomes fully political, going beyond its diffuse pietistic and ethical imperatives and nostalgias. For it is here that the elements in the Islamist repertoire are rendered elements in a specific notion of history, in a specific notion of society, and in a specific notion of political action.

History[18] takes place in two registers, one of which has a decided ontological distinction over the other: the authentic, and the inauthentic; that of the Islamic self, and that of its corruptions by otherness, such as non-Islamic people and religions, schisms, heresies and a manifold of enemies. The one is posited as original, hence necessary and in accord with nature, for Islam is a primeval religion (*dīn al-fiṭra*), and the other is posited as contingent, mere history, the passage of time as sheer succession and pure seriality, bereft of significance, and therefore of quality.

This ontologically differentiated history results in a discourse of absolute specificity and the rejection of any universalistic notions of history or of progress, much like Tolstoy and Mikhailovsky in Russia, and like certain forms for the expression of negritude or other forms of communalist and populist-nationalist expression. History for the highly influential Egyptian Sayyid Quṭb (executed in 1966) is "a memory determined by the authority" of the foundational age of Islam[19] – what we saw to be a utopia. All other history is contingent exoticism, for history that is ontologically weighty is limited to the history of the Islamic ego against which is set an absolute otherness. In principle impermeable, this ego is yet subject to degradation, which is of necessity contingent and solely attributable to exotic ruses and snares: of Manichaean and Muslim schismatics in the Middle Ages, of Jews/Marxists/Masons, allied to the evils of constitutionalism, Arab nationalism and other universal political principles in modernity.

Political Islamism seeks the retrieval of this essence superordinate over mere history; hence the names adopted by Islamist political groups, reminiscent of those adopted by ascendent and subaltern nationalisms: Renaissance (*Nahḍa*, *Risorgimento*), Salvation (*Khalāṣ*), Awakening (*Iḥyā'*, *Yaqaẓa*), and their cognates. The present is a condition of radical degradation and deviance, and the task of the retrieval is the restoration of the pristine order, the primitivist utopia. The present is, at best, a Nicht-Ich, "occidentosis".[20] Absolute Unbelief makes it incumbent upon Islamist political *groupuscules* to shun their contemporaries and to resocialize their members according to the meta-social utopian model as an anti-society, and to condemn absolutely any attempt to "ornament" this utopia or to render it acceptable to modern sensibilities or to formulate it in terms of modern political principles, such as nationalism, liberalism or socialism. Indeed, Islam "regards the way of God and His Law as the fundamental principle to which people should conform, and to which reality must be adapted".[21]

Thus we have a Romantic notion of history which is familiar in modern history – from Herder and his patrimony in Germany, to ideas current in the Risorgimento, to the organicist conservatism of Gustave Le Bon. All these are widely attested to in the history of modern Arab thought, although irrationalism in modern Arab political and social thought has not yet been systematically examined. Indeed, we can also say that there are common conditions of emergence, and that there are convergences between modern Arab irrationalism and European irrationalisms. Islamist irrationalism is a new phenomenon – classical Islamic reformism was a curious mixture of organicist historism and evolutionism, with a liberal-constitutionalist and utilitarian interpretation of the scriptures.[22] Modern political Islamism, a product of the past two and a half decades, was born at a different conjuncture, which allowed it to articulate the elements of the Islamist repertoire with the concept of history available from Arab nationalist ideology, especially its expression in the 1930s and 1940s, associated with Baathism, and clearly formulated with reference to Nietzsche, Spengler, Bergson and others. With the Arab nationalist project defeated and in abeyance, especially after 1967, Islamist political discourse tended in some instances to subsume a hypernationalism in terms of the Islamist repertoire, or at least to bear it in its folds,[23] and indeed to fuse with the sort of nationalist advocacy put forward by a suddenly deeply pious Saddam Hussein in 1990–91. In all cases, the potency of the religious symbolic repertoire was primed into the moulds of nationalist ideology that constitutes the actual political culture of the Arab World.

Islamist political discourse is loath to specify the political system that the Islamic state would create and invigilate. It normally rests content with emphasizing the uniqueness of this society, it being one where God is the sole legislator.[24] Beyond the legal order which re-enacts the primitivist utopia, nothing remains but a savage vitalism: the social order will "emerge vitally" from doctrine, and doctrine becomes "the actual and active reality of the group".[25]

This lack of specification appears odd in the light of the detailed regulation attributed to Islamic law. Yet this silence is not fortuitous, neither is it without cover, and the cover is provided by the vitalist expression often used. Vitalism yields two important consequences: a notion of social homogeneity which implies a corporatist notion of society, and a naturalistic concept of the socio-historical order and of the natural inevitability of the utopian restoration.

Islamist political discourse always insists that the Islamic party is not a political party on a par with other political parties, but that it is distinguished by being consonant with the ontologically privileged history outlined above. It represents the element of continuity, and is therefore above and beyond political dissent, constituting instead the very core of the Being-Social, the median point in an order which, if it were to be in keeping with the ontological privilege of normalcy and in conformity to the nature of things, must be homogeneous, undivided, bereft of difference or of differentiation, an even surface from whence authority and order spring vitally, a surface whose evenness renders possible the direct and unmediated action of political authority. This is amply shown in the attitudes towards democracy adopted by Islamist groups that menace the fledgling democratic processes in, say, Algeria. With a totalitarian valorization of the Rousseauian notion of the General Will, these groups postulate that the accomplishment of democracy can only be signalled when an Islamic state is erected, thus making for the full correspondence of state and society – some Islamists with curious minds or left-wing pasts state this in Gramscian terms, as do members of the growing group of Arab populist nationalists. The rejection of party-political location thus acts as the grid through which the image of the total state is made into a political programme and an agency for totalitarian control, for the pronounced educational function of this state is geared to the total homogenization of cultural and social space. From this Islamist political parties derive their notion of democracy: democracy becomes a totalitarian passion whereby the Islamist party substitutes itself for the body politic, conceived as a social protoplasm which remains formless until it is endowed with an Islamic order.

With the advent of this finalist Islamic polity, it is not only society to which the state is brought in correspondence. This correspondence is based on a sort of pre-established harmony, located in the proposition, mentioned above and universally stated by Islamist authors, that the Islamic order is primeval, in conformity with the predisposition of societies at all times and places, a sort of natural law, or even a cosmic order. For the rule of Islam is inevitable, as humanity must ultimately conform to the role allotted it by the Almighty, and deference to the Word of God in matters of social and political organization is simply a recognition of the sole order of society in conformity with the order of the cosmos.[26] The affinity between this pan-naturalism attributed to the restorative ideology, and the National Socialist cult of nature is manifest.[27] A common condition of emergence could be sought in a classical trope of all ideology, the naturalization of history. Another connection might be sought in Alexis Carrel (d.1944), the fascistoid Frenchman who has so entranced Islamist authors like Quṭb and Shariati,[28] and who, like them, wrote at great length about the degeneracy of modern conditions, the solution to which he found with the neutralization of the proletarian multitude and the revivification of the germoplasm containing the "ancestral potentialities" of the "energetic strains" of North-Western Europe.[29]

Carrel also dwelt at length on the need for an elite – social and biological – for the salvation of civilization.[30] This elite, for Islamist political ideologies, is the group which sets itself apart from society and defends the rights of God as against the rights of mortals, and implements the eternal writ of God as against the unbelieving opinions of men, and which prepares itself for offensive politico-military action that aims at the correction of the world, and bringing it into harmony with the cosmos.[31]

The naturalistic argument for the inevitability of Islamic rule mentioned is not often manifestly deployed, although it is always implicit. Indeed, Sayyid Quṭb, who propounded it, also propounded the position that no arguments from nature or from nationality can buttress the Islamist political position, which must rest on divine command, and this position is even more pronounced amongst Quṭbist groups of the 1970s and 1980s.[32] In other words, the political imperatives do not relate to political conditions, according to this conception.

The most important consequence of this is that the realization of the category of political Islam is a very highly voluntaristic action. It is this voluntarist notion of political action which explains much of the apparent apolitical nihilism that marks the positions of Islamist groups. Direct, unmediated action aims to homogenize the surface of society, or assumes it to be homogeneous; it can be well described in terms of Hegel's analysis of the Absolute Freedom of the Jacobins in the *Phenomenology*. The world is the immediate substance of political action, and this political action is frozen in the moment of pure confrontation and contestation. Needless to say, there is no precedent for this conspiratorial notion of total political action in Muslim tradition. Instead, Islamist political activity stands in direct relation, because of common conditions of emergence in modernity as well as by direct example, to clandestine party organization and the tradition of the élitist *putsch* identified in the twentieth century with Bolshevism and its numerous progeny East and West, and this in turn goes back to the tradition in which gelled Babouvism and Freemasonry at the close of the eighteenth century, which gave rise to the Carbonari and the nineteenth-century revolutionary tradition.

Yet this degree zero of politics, this notion of contestation as total war, this immediate resort to terrorism, this practical end of the restorative concept of history, is the corollary of its beginning. The politicization of the sacred, the sacralization of politics, and the transformation of Islamic pseudo-legal institutes – the tokens of Islamicity – into "social devotions",[33] are all means of realizing the politics of the authentic ego, a politics of identity, and are therefore the means for the very formation, indeed the invention, of this identity. The secret of Islam as a political category lies therein, that the image of the total state is reproduced under the guise of reaffirming a pre-existing identity endowed with an ontological privilege, an identity which is but the nominal node for the interpellation, by nominal association, of a host of tokens. It is this selfsame node of interpellation that constitutes the hinge whereby are articulated the ideological notions of political Islamism – notions of history, the body politic, and of political action – and the tokens which fully stand for Islam. And what this Islam devolves to is the mirror image of the modernist state which originated with the Jacobins, was routinized and historicized in the Napoleonic state, and exported worldwide. The modernism of this proposed state is the fundamental feature of this supposedly pre-modern creature of postmodernism.

Contestation and Democracy

Islamist discourse is therefore a celebrated witness to neo-orientalism, and the deliberate archaism of the former sustains the postmodernism of the latter. It transpired that Islamist political language is far from being *sui generis*; indeed, even if it were, it will still have been communicable, for communication is in fact premised on the non-equivalence of the interlocutors, and no degree of under-determination precludes successful communication, for indeed, it is indeterminacy which is "the measure of information".[34]

If we were to look with sober eyes at the history and politics of this discourse on history and politics, we would find ourselves amid a situation certain features of which have particular salience for our purpose, and I will outline these briefly before turning directly to the connection of all these matters with democracy.

The political origins of this Islamist discourse with its many varieties and inflections are easy to identify. It started in the 1950s and 1960s, as a local Arab purveyance of the Truman Doctrine, and was sustained initially by Egyptian and Syrian Islamists – both earnest ones, and socially conservative, pro-Saudi business and other elements opposed to Nasserism and Baathism. This was indeed the first great cultural and ideological enterprise of Petro-Islam, along with ideas of pan-Islamism as a force counterbalancing Arab nationalism, and Islamic authenticity combatting "alien" ideologies. The idea that religious affiliation is a potent weapon with which to wage war against state structures in the Middle East is not, of course, a new one, and has a history of trying to encourage the matching of religious and political affiliation – the first moment of this was Balkanization, the present one Lebanization.[35]

The Petro-Islamic enterprise has been hugely successful, especially with the substantial influx of the Arab intelligentsia to the relatively backward countries of the Arabian Peninsula, and the colossal ensemble of mediatic and other cultural organs that Petro-Islam has built up, and with which, most importantly, it has broken the secularist and nationalist cultural, mediatic and, to a lesser extent, the educational monopoly of the modern Arab state. It has resulted in the Islamic acculturation of certain social groups: not the recovery of an essence, but the manufacture of an identity. This is why Islamism is a force without resonance in places like the city of Sfax in Tunisia, whose internal economic and social structures seem to be in a good measure of continuity with the recent past, but with substantial influence in a city like Tunis, where sections of the population were traumatized by forces of social pulverization.[36]

On the basis of this hegemonic project, Islamism is now laying claims, like those countenanced for it by neo-orientalism, to the representation of the body politic – a surface construed to be as even as that of "Islamic" society. It may be remembered that prior to the municipal elections in Algeria in June 1990, Abbasi Madani, the leader (now encarcerated) of the so-called National Salvation Front, said that he was confident of victory, and threatened untold violence and terror in case of disappointment. Apart from an attempt to terrorize state and electorate, the implicit assumption is that defeat of the Islamists would represent an act so unnatural that speech fails, and the only answer to which would have to be the "non-discursive" assertion of nature, the self-realization of a transcendental narcissism. This pseudo-sociological notion of correspondence between Arab society and Islamist polity is now a central feature of the Islamist discourse on democracy and seems to sustain itself in an exclusively plebiscitary notion of democracy – democracy as a totalitarian passion for the identity of state and society, the liberal democratic form being the prelude to the abolition of liberal democracy.

This was not, of course, always so. The "Islamic liberalism" which we saw advocated above, more than half a century out of phase, had a creative interpretation of Islam in terms of constitutionalism, rather than the other way round as is the case today. This consisted of a liberal exegetical effort, toward the Koran as well as early Islamic tradition, with a view to producing a concordance between the sense of this textual body and democratic ideas and institutions. This, in the work of Muhammad Abduh (d.1905) and others, was part of a modernist reinterpretation of Muslim texts of sacred or semi-sacred character, in which these texts were regarded as a code, open to the modernist interpreter, which yielded ideas in keeping with science, with evolutionism, and other ideas in currency, including nineteenth-century European attitudes of sexual propriety. There were similar movements in the history of Catholicism, particularly in eighteenth-century France, and certainly before the influence of Bonald and Lamennais made itself felt. But this effort depends on an epistemological *legerdemain*, which operates by assuming the scriptures do not mean what they say. And this bluff was called by the ascendant fundamentalist Islam, in the past two decades, and the time for Muslim liberalism has certainly passed, although it still has many voices, some of them very creative and of considerable talent, but the most important of which is the Arab state, which has embraced Islamic modernism as its own.

So the question of democracy in the Arab World, as elsewhere, in countries with Muslim majorities and other parts of the South, is located elsewhere, beyond the bounds of mystification and within the boundaries of history and of politics: not as the realization of the Truth of society. Sectarianism is a sub-species of communalism, and communalism, a political phenomenon, is far more than the sheer register of the social and historical existence of communities. As in the liberal pluralism of Britain in the early part of this century, the liberal democratic position in the Arab World is formulated in opposition to the idealist theory of the state as coextensive with society and to the concomitant organicist paradigm of society I have outlined.

It is a fact that, despite claims of neo-orientalists and Islamists alike, Arab countries are subject to the social, cultural, political and ideological forms which, in the past two centuries, have become universal, albeit with varying rhythms, articulations and determinations. We have seen Islamism itself partaking of universality in its claims for specificity and irreducibility, with a pronounced sense of kinship to generic fascism and right-wing forms of subaltern nationalism; in Europe, it acts as a counter-fascism. This universalism is inescapable. Of European origin undoubtedly, expanding throughout the world by colonial and neo-colonial transformation of economies, societies, polities and cultures, this universalism leaves nothing intact, for the universal history of modernity is a voracious consumer of particularities. It brings together in this global concatenation even the most bizarre and archaic sectors of society and culture, whose abiding archaism – or, rather, I should say archaization, traditionalization – is their mode of contemporaneity in this global combined and uneven development, and provides a "real time" ideological sustenance to political philo-Islamism in the West, a latter-day "indirect rule" instrument. We cannot underestimate the role of Western mediatic representation in this archaization: exotic, marginal religious manifestations are presented as central, civil wars or insurrections which have political and other causes are presented persistently as sectarian – and these representations are transmitted back to their countries of origin, at once distorting realities, and actively inciting sectarian conflicts.

It goes without saying that unevenness is not confined to peripheries – European societies themselves form very uneven social, cultural and religious surfaces. There is no need to think of some particularly generic exotic quality in terms of which democracy in the Arab World should be understood or practised. This is so not because there is nothing specific there, for the banal truth is that everything is specific. Nor is it the case that there is a constant copying of matters European, although this copying indeed takes place. Universalism is quite simply the participation, *volens nolens*, in a historical movement which, though Western European in origin, is now a global patrimony. Its insertion in the peripheries is incomplete and uneven, because of the weak institution of social and cultural formation, a weakness which is the counterpart of "authentic" assertiveness. There is no culturally specific theory of democracy, as there is no epistemology specific for studying others, except exoticism, whose epistemology I have outlined above; for the determinants of all knowledge are historical, not "cultural".

The conditions of democracy in Arab lands are therefore a matter to be seen in the light of social and political conditions generally, and in the light of the presence of blockages, not specific to the Arab World, which produce Islamist politics: in political, social, economic and normative conflicts, in the heterogeneity and weak institution of society and culture, in the constitution and reconstitution of variant identities, including secular nationalism, liberal and authoritarian, and of the various groups of the intelligentsia. The conditions of democracy should also be sought in the state: the state itself, in some instances such as Morocco, Jordan, Yemen, Algeria, Tunisia and Egypt, has been the agency which, with imperfections and varying trajectories, has lately promoted forms of democracy. In some cases (Jordan and Algeria) this was the sign of the state abdicating its political and educational functions and throwing a society, traumatized into the opium of Islamism, to an uncertain future. In other cases, a good measure of political rationality dictated political transformations towards democracy, however imperfect, provisional, or reticent – a rationality responding to growing public political awareness, to the capacity for political organization, to increasing concatenations of "civil society", both by the *Bildungsbürgertum* so important in modern Arab history, as by a talismanic aspect that democracy is acquiring in the eyes of Arabs, as an element guarding against future calamities.

Democracy in the Arab World therefore is not a mysterious matter to be unravelled by neo-orientalist expertise. It has nothing to do with "identity", except in so far as it will add *citizenship* in the proper sense to the web of multiple identities that mark all individuals and collectivities everywhere and at all times, thereby completing the transition from communal to civil society. This process, like all historical processes, is highly conflictual. Islamist politics is one party to this conflict, a party which seeks to drain politics out of society and confine it to the state. And we have seen that, this being the case, Islamist politics, with its combination of "pre-Galilean consciousness and post-Hegelian discourse",[37] is an eminently historical player subject to the ruse of history.

Notes

1. David Harvey, *The Condition of Postmodernity. An Inquiry into the Origins of Cultural Change*, Oxford 1989, chs 10, 11 and passim.

2. Etienne Balibar, "*Es Gibt keinen Staat in Europa*: Racism and Politics in Europe Today", *New Left Review* 186, 1991, pp. 10ff.

3. I.C. Jarvie, *Rationality and Relativism. In Search of a Philosophy and History of Anthropology*, London 1984, passim.

4. Ernesto Laclau, *New Reflections on the Revolution of our Time*, London 1991, pp. 17–18.

5. J.M. Lotman, "On the Metalanguage of a Typological Description of Culture", *Semiotica*, 14/2, 1975, pp. 97ff.

6. In France: G. Kepel, *Le Prophète et Pharaon*, Paris 1984 (transl J. Rothschild, as *The Prophet and Pharaoh*, London 1985); in the Anglo-Saxon World and Israel: E. Sivan, *Radical Islam: Medieval Theology and Modern Politics*, New Haven and London 1985.

7. A. Al-Azmeh, *Islamic Studies and the European Imagination*, Exeter 1986; this volume, ch. 7.

8. For a concrete corrective, see E. Davis, "The Concept of Revival and the Study of Islam and Politics", in Barbara Freyer Stowasser, ed., *The Islamic Impulse*, London 1987, pp. 37–58.

9. Kepel, *Prophet and Pharaoh*; and O. Carré, *Les Frères Musulmans*, Paris 1983.

10. L. Binder, *Islamic Liberalism. A Critique of Development Ideologies*, Chicago and London 1988, pp. 358–9.

11. Ibid, p.1.

12. Kepel, *Prophet and Pharaoh*, p. 225.

13. Al-Azmeh, *Islamic Studies and the European Imagination*; and "Ifṣāḥ al-istishrāq", in A. Al-Azmeh, *Al-Turāth bayn al-sulṭān wa'l-tārīkh*, Casablanca and Beirut 1987, pp. 61ff.

14. Al-Azmeh, "Utopia and Islamic Political Thought", *History of Political Thought*, XI/I, 1990, pp. 91ff and this volume, ch. 5; and *Al-Kitaba al-tārīkhiya wa'l-ma'rifa al-tararikhiya*, Beirut 1983, pp. 93ff.

15. The above is based on Al-Azmeh, *Al-Turāth*, pp. 51ff. Cf. M.

Arkoun, *Ouvertures sur l'Islam*, Paris 1989, p. 46, who, following Lyotard, speaks of the "degradation" of signs to symbols.

16. E. Laclau, *Politics and Ideology in Marxist theory*, London 1979, p. 194.

17. D. MacRae, "Populism as an Ideology", in E. Gellner and G. Ionescu, eds, *Populism. Its Meaning and National Characteristics*, London 1969, pp. 155–6. The connection between Islamism and populism is also noted by E. Abrahamian, "Khomeini: Fundamentalist or Populist", *New Left Review* 186, 1991, pp. 102–19.

18. See Al-Azmeh, "The Discourse of Cultural Authenticity", in E. Deutsch, ed., *Culture and Modernity*, Honolulu 1991, pp. 468ff; and this volume, ch. 2.

19. M.H. Diyāb, *Sayyid Quṭb. Al-Khiṭāb wa'l-Idyulūjīyā*, Beirut 1988, p. 105.

20. The title of a book by the Iranian Islamist cultural critic, Jalal Al-i Ahmad, *Occidentosis. A Plague from the West*, transl. R. Campbell, Berkeley 1984.

21. S. Quṭb, *Maʿālim fi't-ṭarīq*, Cairo and Beirut 1981, pp. 41–2, 189, and passim; and the text of Islamist terrorist leaders in R. Sayyid Aḥmad, *Al-Nabī al-musallaḥ*, London 1990, vol. 1, pp. 40–42, 53–103, 130, 148–9 and passim.

22. One can usefully consult A. Laroui, *Islam et modernité*, Paris 1987, pp. 127ff, and A. Al-Azmeh, "Islamic Revivalism and Western Ideologies", *History Workshop Journal*, 32, 1991, pp. 44ff, and this volume, ch. 4. On irrationalism in modern Arab thought generally, see Raif Khuri, *Modern Arab Thought*, transl. I. Abbas, Princeton 1983, and Aziz Al-Azmeh, *Al-ʿIlmānīya*, Beirut 1992, passim.

23. A. Al-Azmeh, "Islamism and Arab Nationalism", *Review of Middle East Studies*, 4, 1988, pp. 33ff, and this volume, ch. 3.

24. For example, Ayatollah Khomeini, *Al-Ḥukūma al-islāmīyya*, Beirut 1979, p. 41.

25. Quṭb, *Maʿālim*, pp. 43–5; and, *Al-Mustaqbal li-hādhā al-dīn*, Cairo n.d., p. 12.

26. Quṭb, *Maʿālim*, pp. 53, 110–11; and *Al-Islām wa mushkilāt al-ḥaḍāra*, n.p. 1968, pp. 4–5.

27. See R. Pois, *National Socialism and the Religion of Nature*, London 1986, pp. 38–44 and passim.

28. Quṭb, *Al-Islam*, pp. 7–30, 108 and passim; A. Shariati, *Marxism and Other Western Fallacies*, transl. R. Campbell, Berkeley 1986, pp. 15–16. See the detailed apologetic biography by R. Soupault, *Alexis Carrel*, Paris 1952. The connection between Quṭb and Carrel has also been discussed by Y. Choueiri, *Islamic Fundamentalism*, London 1990, pp. 142–9.

29. A. Carrel, *Man the Unknown*, West Drayton, Middlesex 1948, pp. 252–4, 276 and passim.

30. Ibid., pp. 271–3, 277.

31. Quṭb, *Maʿālim*, pp. 11–12, 20, 72ff.

32. Quṭb, *Naḥwa mujtamaʿ islāmī*, Beirut 1980, p. 11; Sayyid Aḥmad, *Al-Nabī*, vol. 1, pp. 127–9.

33. The term comes from the Muslim Brother cleric M. Ghazālī, *Min hunā naʿlam*, Cairo 1954, p. 44.

34. Y.M. Lotman, *Universe of the Mind. A Semiotic Theory of Culture*, London 1990, p. 227.

35. G. Corm, *L'Europe et l'Orient de la balcanisation à la libanisation. Histoire d'une modernité inaccomplie*, Paris 1989.

36. M.A. Hirmāsī, "Al-Islām al-iḥtijājī fī Tūnis", in *Al-Ḥarakāt al-Islāmīyya al-muʿāṣira*, Beirut 1987, pp. 249ff.

37. D. Shayeghan, *Le Regard mutilé*, Paris 1989; Arabic translation as *Al-Nafs al-mabtūra*, London 1991, pp. 77, 89–90, 95–6.

2

The Discourse of Cultural Authenticity: Islamist Revivalism and Enlightenment Universalism

I take it as an accomplished fact that modern history is characterized by the globalization of the Western order. Despite protests of a bewildering variety against this accomplished fact, it remains incontestable, especially as, with few exceptions of an isolated and purely local nature, these protests have taken place either in the name of ideologies of Western provenance – such as national independence and popular sovereignty – or substantially in terms of these ideologies, albeit symbolically beholden to a different local or specific repertory, such as the Iranian regime of the Ayatollahs. The validation of universalism does not arise from some transcendental or immanent criterion, but quite simply from affirming the rationality of the real.

The reasons for this are manifest: the conditions of Western economic and political conquest and hegemony in the modern age have engendered, for good or for ill, correlative conditions of equally real ideological and cultural hegemony. The East – and I only use this term for convenience – has been heavily impregnated with novel categories of thought, methods of education, contents of knowledge, forms of discourse and communication, aesthetic norms and ideological positions. It has become impossible to speak with sole reference to traditional texts and without reference to Western notions.

There is nothing particularly mysterious about this irreversible state of affairs, and the conditions for cross-cultural knowledge are not distinct from the conditions of knowledge in general. A cross-cultural epistemology is neither possible nor desirable. Knowledge is always of an object, and in this view the quiddity of other cultures is not substantially distinct from the objectness of any other object of knowledge – knowledge being empirical, aesthetic, historical, and its objects therefore being appropriate for these modes of apprehension and reason. Culture is a very coy object and is a term rather thoughtlessly applied to objects poorly apprehended or regarded as somewhat exotic and quaint.

One would therefore be better advised to speak of a universal civilization comprising a manifold of historical formations – the European, the Arab, the Indian. Each of these is highly differentiated, but these differences, or the cluster of such differences, are globally articulated and unified by the economic, political, cultural and ideological facts of dominance. Each historical unit is, moreover, multivocal, and Europe of course is no exception to this, despite the claims that are made on behalf of a triumphalist Hegelianism, somewhat impoverished by the elimination from it of history.

In this light, the notion of incommensurability and its cognates appears quite absurd, not only because historical units are not analogous to paradigms and apprehension is not analogous to translation. Neither are they homogeneous, self-enclosed and entirely self-referential entities, as would be required by the assumption of univocal irreducibility. The consequences of such assumptions exceed the simple elision of history and lead to a barren and naïve relativist temptation with at best a patronizing rhetoric of intercultural etiquette dressed up as a philosophical hermeneutic. More perniciously it leads to the absolute relativism that underlies apartheid and the culturalist pretensions of some political groups such as those that came to prominence with the conjuration of the Salman Rushdie affair.

This compulsory universalism can be illustrated with a particular case made all the more poignant because it is an advocacy of exclusivism and of incommensurable distinction. I have indicated that Europe has everywhere spawned ideological and cultural phenomena as diverse as her own. What appears in the East under the guise of traditionalism is normally an apologetic or a radically reformist discourse whose terms of articulation and criteria of validation are by no means traditional – traditions do not validate themselves, they are idioms. There are indeed deliberate archaisms and medievalisms that may appear in direct continuity with the past. Among these I would class the cultivation, for the purposes other than recondite antiquarianism and historical research, of such matters as the magnificently ornate re-paganized Neoplatonism in vogue in Iran. This naturally evokes a chilling sense of the Gothic, but could with some effort be made comprehensible in historical conditions over-determined by European modernity. For it is a fact of the modern history of the Arab World, or of Iran and other countries with Muslim majorities – and it should be strongly emphasized that Islam is not a culture, but a religion living amidst very diverse cultures and thus a very multiform entity – that the predominant literate discourses in social and political life are local adaptations of Enlightenment and post-Enlightenment traditions, such as Marxism, naturalism, liberalism and nationalism.

In what follows, an attempt will be made to anatomize a notion of much potency in modern Arab social and political thought: it is hoped that a paradigm that will make comparable other exclusivist ideologies increasingly at work in the world, such as right-wing Hindu communalism, Zionist fundamentalism both secular and religious, and much else, will become explicit.

I

In common with other subaltern nationalisms, as with defensive, retrenching nationalisms and with populist ideologies, the notion of authenticity is widely used both in formal discourse on matters political and social and in the interstices of casual comment. The notion of authenticity is not so much a determinate concept as it is a node of associations and interpellations, a trope by means of which the historical world is reduced to a particular order, and a token which marks off social and political groups and forges and reconstitutes historical identities. In these senses the notion of authenticity has analogues elsewhere, doubtless officiated under different names.

Aṣāla is the Arabic term for authenticity. Lexically, it indicates salutary moral qualities like loyalty, nobility, and a sense of commitment to a specific social group or a set of values. It also indicates a sense of *sui generis* originality; and in association with the senses previously mentioned, *aṣāla* specifically refers to genealogical standing: noble or at least respectable descent for humans, and the status of equine aristocrats. Combined together and transferred to an attribute of historical collectivities, Arab, Muslim or other, *aṣāla* becomes a central notion in a Romantic conception of history which calls forth features commonly associated with such a conception. Of primary importance among these features is a vitalist concept of nationalism and of politics, replete with biological metaphor and, occasionally, a sentimentalist populism.

Ultimately, therefore, the notion of authenticity is predicated on the notion of a historical subject which is at once self-sufficient and self-evident. Its discourse is consequently an essentialist discourse, much like the reverse it finds in Orientalism, in discourses on the primitive, and in other discourses on cultural otherness.[1] In common with these discourses, the discourse on authenticity postulates a historical subject which is self-identical, essentially in continuity over time, and positing itself in essential distinction from other historical subjects. For the viability of a historical subject such as this, it is essential that its integrity must be maintained against a manifest backdrop of change of a very rapid and profound nature. It therefore follows that change should be conceived as contingent, impelled by inessential matters like external interference or internal subversion, the effects of which can only be faced with a reassertion of the essence of historical subjectivity. History therefore becomes an alternance in a continuity of decadence and health, and historiographical practice comes to consist in the writing of history as a form of classification of events under the two categories of intrinsic and extrinsic, the authentic and the imputed, the essential and the accidental.

It is therefore not fortuitous or haphazard that the title under whose name this discourse (and its political implications) is officiated should be revivalism, *nahḍa*, in line with similar historical and ideological experiences of which the *Risorgimento* readily comes to mind. For this entire ideological trope can be described as one of ontological irredentism, it being the attempt to retrieve an essence that the vicissitudes of time and the designs of enemies, rather than change of any intrinsic nature, had caused to atrophy. The counterpart of this was that the degraded conditions of today are mere corruptions of the original cultural essence, the retrieval of which is only possible by a return to the pristine beginnings which reside in the early years of Islam, the teachings of the book of God, the Koran, and the example of the Prophet Muhammad. It must be added at the outset, however, that though revivalism was initially Islamist, and has tended to don the Islamist cloak in the very recent past, it received its most thorough grounding in the context of secular Arab nationalist ideology, which regarded Islam as but one moment of Arab glory, albeit an important one.

In historical terms, this constellation of notions came into currency in the second half of the nineteenth century, first with the Young Ottomans in Istanbul, and particularly Namik Kemal (1840–88), and shortly thereafter in the writings of the remarkable Jamāl al-Dīn al-Afghānī (1839–97). Afghānī was not a profound thinker, but a very potent speaker and charismatic conspirator. His careers in Istanbul, Tehran, Kabul, Hyderabad, Calcutta, Cairo, London, Paris and St Petersburg have left an important imprint on pan-Islamism in the Arab World, which, in certain respects at his time, can be regarded as a form of protonationalism.[2] Afghānī left a body of miscellaneous writings, most notably his polemic against the pro-British Indian Muslim reformer Sir Syed Ahmad Khan (1817–98),[3] with whose ideas, it must be stressed, he was not really at variance. He inspired the journal *Al-ʿUrwa al-wuthqā*, a collaborative body of political, cultural and reformist writing published in Paris in 1882–83 with his then disciple, Muhammad ʿAbduh (1849–1905), who was later to become the Arab World's foremost and most subtle Muslim reformist.[4] A section of ʿAbduh's writings are in tune with the general theses of Afghānī, but are far more finely tuned and retain none of Afghānī's occasional crudeness of conception, and ʿAbduh's disciples numbered some of the Arab World's foremost Muslim reformist and nationalist leaders in the early part of this century. This same constellation of notions was channelled into the mainstream of Arab political and social thought through the nationalism which was later to become Turkish nationalism exemplified in Ziya Gökalp (1875–1924) and the Arab nationalism of his erstwhile associate, Satiʿ al-Husri (1880–1968),[5] although Husri was not a Romantic revivalist and populist like Gökalp, and Romantic revivalism was only to enter Arab nationalism between the wars, a process to which Husri, though at the peak of his career, was far too sober a positivist sociologist and educationist to contribute.

Before describing the anatomy of the notion of authenticity, it will be well to make a number of further historical specifications. It was rare after Afghānī for Islamist revivalism to take the Romantic form until very recently; its revivalism was concentrated on the revivification of a utopia which consisted of a clear set of precedents of a social, legal and moral order unconnected with an elaborate notion of history. It was only when Islamism associated itself with nationalism – the prevalent ideological impulse in the Arab World – and assimilated it in such a way that Islamism became a viable medium for the articulation of nationalism, that Islamism became Romantic and returned to the tropes of Jamāl al-Dīn al-Afghānī, who is idolized by today's Islamists. Finally, it must be stressed that it is extremely difficult to study precisely how Afghānī or his acolytes became Romantic. The notion of authenticity, which will be described presently, lies at the intersection of a number of concepts that are foreign to classical Islamic thought, which constituted the core of Afghānī's education. It is well known that the highlights of European thought were becoming quite familiar in Cairo, Istanbul and elsewhere from the early part of the nineteenth century and that they contributed to the formation of Young Ottoman thought.[6] But I believe it to be impossible philologically to trace European influence from such quarters of paramount importance for the notion of authenticity as Herder and the German historical school of law associated with Savigny and others at any time before about 1930, although some French thinkers in a roughly similar vein, such as Gustave Le Bon, were fairly well known.[7] If influence there was, it would most probably have come orally or implicitly in the body of occasional writing such as journalism; it is also very important to study the social and political conditions under which Romantic nationalism (or proto-nationalism) could grow spontaneously.

II

The nation for Afghānī is akin to a body, and although he changed his mind over what constituted a nation, in the final analysis he devalued ties of ethnicity and, to a lesser extent, of language to the advantage of the bond of religion.[8] A nation consists of estates analogous to parts of a body, or of individuals whose organic unity is that of the parts of a vital organism. This organism is infused with a vital force like that which permeates its individual organs, and the power of this individual vitality is directly proportional to that in the whole organism.[9]

This organismic, vitalist paradigm has its major notions – if not its object, a socio-political order – in medieval Islamic natural philosophy. Equally important is that it naturally invites comparison with Herder's notion of *Kräfte* as inner sources of vitality and dynamic principles for the continued existence of nations; the question as to whether Herder's Romanticism is medieval in its conceptual inspiration is irrelevant to its modernity and to the vital part it played in nineteenth- and twentieth-century ideological tendencies. Though Afghānī's ideas initially were shaped in Iranian seminaries, they were received in Calcutta, Cairo, Istanbul and Paris, where they were filtered through contemporary social and political categories. Also like Herder's, Afghānī's paradigm concretizes this vital principle for the unity and cohesion of bodies national in culturalist terms and, like Herder's emphasis on *Bildung*, finds in civic and moral education the key to the maintenance and resuscitation of national glory. The vital spirit in empirical terms is a yearning in the hearts of men for glory and a leaning towards the consummate realization of values. And this vital spirit is operative only when it impels bodies national with a desire for excellence and distinction in wealth as well as glory and might (*ʿizz*).[10]

In situations of conflict brought about by pervasive Western interference in the Middle East, this perspective was not unnaturally invested with a social-Darwinist stance. It is well to bear in mind that the "conflict theory" of political sociology was emerging in Germany at about the same time – proponents of this theory, as well as Afghānī, were keenly interested in Ibn Khaldūn's theory of the power of state, which they used in the construction of a nationalist Romanticism.[11] The struggle for existence, Afghānī tells us, pervades human history no less than in the animal kingdom and inanimate nature. The reason for this is that "might is the visible aspect of life and of continued existence ... and might is never triumphant and concrete except when it weakens and subjugates others." As illustration, Afghānī cites the powers of nations, and specifically the subjugation of the Ottoman Empire by the European powers.[12]

What, in this perspective, is history? And what does the passage of time yield? It can be noted that the subject of history is the body national. Each body national, as in Herder, is a fixed nature which is, according to the characterization of Collingwood, less the product of history than its presupposition.[13] That unit which is historically significant is the national subject, and history is therefore one of alternance between true historicity manifested in might, and historical desuetude manifested in subjugation. Might results from cohesiveness and unity, and if this unity were to be lost the body national would lose its spirit or its general will, with the result that "the thrones of its might will fall, and it [the nation] will take its leave of existence just as existence has abandoned it."[14] It is indicative of Afghānī's style that he used the term *quwwa ḥāfiẓa*, which I have rendered as "spirit". The expression, literally "preservative power", is derived from medieval Arabic natural philosophy, in which Afghānī was deeply steeped and concepts from which he often used, where it designates the subliminal quality which keeps together a somatic composite.

The cohesiveness and unity of this body national infused with a vital impulse that yearns for glory is maintained so long as the factors which originally constituted this *Volksgeist* are operative. But once corruption sets in, once the essence is diluted, the auguries of national calamity become manifest. Thus the glorious classical civilization of the Muslim Arabs was corroded from the inside by the snares of esotericist sects, which paved the way for conquest by Crusaders and Mongols. Similarly, the fabric of the Ottoman Empire was weakened by Ottoman westernizing reformists in the middle of the nineteenth century. As for the French, the glory of their royal past was corrupted by the seductions of Voltaire and Rousseau, which directly led to what Afghānī regarded as the calamities of the French Revolution, the Paris Commune and defeat in the Franco–Prussian War. In the same class of universally destructive, disintegrative impulses are socialism, communism and anarchism, which might cause the annihilation of humanity altogether, being the ultimate forces of corruption and radical antinomianism, the antithesis of order and civilization.[15]

There is no response to weakness and destruction save that of revivalism: the retrieval and restoration of the original qualities that made for strength and historical relevance. No progress without the retrieval of pristine beginnings and the cleansing of the essence from the adulteration of history:[6] such is the fundamental principle of revivalism; the example of Martin Luther was never far from the mind of Afghānī. The Islam that results from the elision of history and the deprivation of time of any significant ontological weight will shortly be taken up; but before this is done it is necessary to take a closer look at the categories that subsist in the trope of authenticity, of absolute individuality and irreducible historical subjectivity.

III

The trope of authenticity described above as less a determinant concept than a node of associations is premised on a number of important notions and distinctions. Fundamental among these is a conception of history which posits a narcissistic continuing subject, mighty by virtue of its nature but enfeebled by subversion, inadvertence and what Hegel termed "Oriental ease and repose". This same subject will regain its vital energy and continue the maintenance of its nature – its entelechy – by a recommencement and by the revivication of its beginnings, which still subsist within it just as a nature, in the classical and medieval Arabic and European senses, inheres in a body.

But this subject is inconceivable in isolation from others, which exist alongside it, for the notion is essentially formed in the context of political contestation. These others are, to a very considerable degree, absolute in their otherness, in that they are antitheses of the subject, and, in order for them to be met, their subjectivity has constantly to be objectified, deprived of value except for that which, like forces of corruption, is inessential and contingent, hence transferable. Such was the attitude of Afghānī and all those who adopted the hopes associated with his name towards modern science and technology, of European provenance but not culture-specific and, moreover, necessary for the construction of national might. Throughout, the origin – the positive beginning – is adulterated, but still flows as a subliminal impulse amid degradation and corruption, for the fall from previous heights is inessential, and the essence of this historical subject is in fact suprahistorical and still subsists in the innermost core of the cultural self. The revivalist project is simply one in which this core is again brought to the surface and to the forefront of historical existence, thereby restoring the historical subject to its true nature.

The truth of this nature is an ontological truth, one whose resistance to the vagaries of time is demonstrated by the revivalist belief in its capacity for resuscitation, and whose durability is the measure of its truth. Indeed, this nature, the vital impulse of the body national, is the very reality of the subject in history; corruption is conceivable only as privation. In the light of this, history consists of continuity over a time which knows no substantive causalities, for causality is only manifest in discontinuity.[17] This continuity is in a constantly antithetical relation to all otherness: to other nations, which by virtue of the very nature of bodies naturally seek to subjugate the nation-subject, and to corruptions within, for these are privations of the essence which seek to subvert, and thus to nullify, the vital energy which uplifts and allows for glory.

Time is therefore cleft between origins and corruptions, between authenticity and the snares of enemies. Forces of privation, of foreign – that is, inessential – provenance, have no intrinsic extensions: they do not extend to the core of the historical self, for they have no avenues that lead to the fund of subjectivity, either in the past or in the present. They have bearings neither in the past nor in the ontological reality of the present. In contrast, extraneous influences disturb the homogeneity of the subject and confound the bearings of its historical course by repudiating the original inner indistinctness and homogeneity which constitute the stuff of authenticity.

Authenticity, for a contemporary philosopher who has been attempting a left-wing reclamation of Afghānī along the lines of a Muslim liberation theology, designates the self in contradistinction to the other, the essential as against the accidental, the natural as opposed to the artificial. Only thus can individuality and specificity properly be said to designate any genuine distinctiveness in opposition to "the loss of distinctiveness and dissolution in another specificity [of the West] which claims universality." Authenticity and its associated notions are, further, said to extend the cultural ego into history and endow it with "historical continuity and temporal homogeneity and the unity of the national personality."[18]

Authenticity is therefore both past and future linked contingently by the ontological void of today. The past is the accomplished future and the future is the past reasserted; history is the past in the future anterior. History is an even continuum, on the surface of which eddy tiny circuits which counter the original energies of the continuum and work to suppress them, yet do not quite succeed in more than rippling the surface and disturbing its evenness. Only thus can teleology be assured: for a nature to consummate itself, for the future revival to close the circle of historical appearance and coalesce with the original condition, the end must be pre-given and inevitable in the sense that it is in accord with nature.

The body national is thus neither describable nor recognizable if measured against its contingent existence, or against the sheer temporality and lack of perfection which characterize it today. Time is devoid of quality, corruption is purely vicarious, and the present is but a negative interregnum between a perfect origin and its recommencement, which is also its consummation. History therefore takes place in "two modes of time, one of which has a decided ontological distinction,"[19] the one relevant to the essence and a measure of its duration, and the other which dissolves into transience and contingency. The former is much like the time of myth as described by Schelling in his *Philosophie der Mythologie*, one which is "indivisible by nature and absolutely identical, which therefore, whatever duration may be imputed to it, can only be regarded as a moment, i.e. as time in which the end is like the beginning and the beginning like the end, a kind of eternity, because it is in itself not a sequence of time."[20]

The connection of these modes of time is the same as that of different bodies national: a connection of otherness which, in a social-Darwinist world, is one of subjugation and of antinomy, essentially of negation, without the possibility of a mutual interiorization such as that inherent in, for example, the Hegelian dialectic of master and slave. Indeed, the polar structuration of the discourse on authenticity is what makes it possible not only to deny essential change in time, thus denying multiplicity over time, but also to deny what we might term spatial multiplicity of any essential consequence, this being the social, political and ideological multiplicity at any one particular point in time, except in so far as such multiplicity is perceived as subversive of a homogeneous essence which requires evenness. Any unevenness, as has already been indicated, is perceived in terms of antithesis, privation, corruption, atrophy.

It goes without saying that, in the real world, this national subject, an essence which knows neither dysfunction nor transformation but only abeyance, must reassert itself against history. Hence it must bring in train an acute sense of voluntarism. If human history is not to be assimilated to that of brute nature, the only agency capable of restoring nature to its course and directing it to the consummation of its entelechy is the will of the reformer, who stands to his nation as does a physician to a body in distemper.[21] And since this body, the body national, is arbitrarily posited as *sui generis*, it follows that the liberty of the reformer can best be described by following the Hegelian analysis of Jacobinism: it is one possessed by a freedom based on pure self-identity, for which the world is its own will, and whose relation to the reality of the world is unmediated, and therefore one of pure negation.[22]

This will, in a pure, indeterminate element, is pure thought of its own self.[23] It is pure self-reference, a tautological circle, whose impenetrability to reason other than the reason of its own self-reference is very much in keeping with similar outlooks in the German *Lebensphilosophie* of the turn of the century, where life is at once the subject and the object of the mind.[24] The crazed waft of blood in the Rushdie affair is fully accounted for in this context. The authentic self is immediately apprehended,[25] and knowledge of it by its own is a sort of pure and perfect *Verstehen*, an almost innate endowment in the mind of the components that make up this body national, whose self-enclosure is epistemological and not only ontological. Indeed, the epistemological and the ontological correspond perfectly, for knowledge of authenticity is but a moment in the life of this authenticity. For what is such knowledge of a self-identical entity but a form of transcendental narcissism? Indeed, Afghānī specifically designates the *Bildung* of the renascent nation as one whose prime medium is an oratory which exhorts and reminds of the past.[26]

It should be clear from the foregoing that the subject being corrected by oratorical education, and which is Romantically conceived both beyond history and underlying it, is indeterminate if its conception is left as presented. There are no indications towards its determination except gestures towards historical particularities: events, names, dates. Beyond this there is reference to a name: Islam. There are analogues to this Romantic mode in virtually all cultures. In all these cases, in the absence of historical determination over and above the indication of a Golden Age wherein inhere exemplary glories and utopian exemplars, the discourse of authenticity is socially open, in the sense that its essential emptiness, what Hegel might have termed the boredom of its concepts, renders it very versatile and protean. As this ontological self-identity is epistemologically reflected in solipsism, the result is that the construction of identities here is fundamentally an act of naming.

Naming is not an innocent activity, but lies at the very heart of ideology, one of whose principal mechanisms is the operation of classificatory tokens that determine the memberships of socio-political groups. These operations also entail exclusions and inclusions by way of condensations, displacements and associative interpellation of some complexity.[27] The concrete images put forward as factually paradigmatic – the golden age, the glories of the Arabs, the Middle Ages in some European Romanticisms, the idyllic rusticity of Heidegger, of African nativist philosophers, or westernized Indian sages – serve as iconic controllers of identities and take on general values generated by a truncated and telescoped history; yet these are values which act as carriers of general attributes that no human collectivity can eternally possess and of paradigmatic value that is only imputed to them by the purveyors of the ideological messages.[28] The versatility of the general name – such as Islam – lies therein; the abstract act of naming engenders as many distinct identities as there are constituted social and political groups which might claim the name as their own. The reality of the historical subject lies not in the head but in historical reality, and the key to this reality is not the conformity to some self-subsistent essence or some invariant historical Islam which does not exist, but the group which adopts the name by adapting it to its particular form and understanding of the historical paradigm evoked by the name, a paradigm which is metonymically suggested and not specifically indicated by the name itself. The connection between name and historical reality derives its validation and credibility from extrinsic criteria, from the capacity that the group adopting the name has to enforce and consolidate its interpretation and to perpetuate it within institutions both epistemic and social.

IV

This elaborate anti-Enlightenment philosophy of history and of politics which has been read from Afghānī's writings and which was constructed largely with the conceptual apparatus of pre-critical philosophy is not the only one which could legitimately be attributed to him. There are strands of other orientations as well. In his response to Renan's famous pronouncements of 1883 about the congenital incapacities of the Semitic mind and the inability of the Arab to produce science and philosophy, Afghānī insisted instead that responsibility for the decline of the brilliant civilization of the Arabs was to be borne entirely by Islam. "It is clear," he wrote, "that wherever it becomes established, this religion tried to stifle the sciences and it was marvelously served in its designs by despotism."

Islam, he added, is not unique in this respect; all religions are intolerant and inimical to reason, and the progress that the West had manifestly achieved was accomplished despite Christianity.[29]

Freethinking of this kind might be accounted for by many factors, not the least of which was that Afghānī led many lives. An Arabic translation of his reply to Renan was deliberately stalled by his then adept Muhammad ʿAbduh. But in order properly to appreciate the legacy of Afghānī's anti-Enlightenment polemic in its full extent, aspects of which will be taken up presently, it is important to draw attention to one other dimension of his position on Renan. For just as he said that Europe progressed despite Christianity, he also said that the Muslims cannot be denied a similar outcome in the achievement of excellence in science and philosophy despite the heavy burden of Islam.[30] The answer, which he never gave in the text of his reply to Renan, was reformism.

The Islam he attacked was the traditional Islam of the ecclesiastics. Like Luther, whom he greatly admired, Afghānī can be said to have "overcome the bondage of piety by replacing it by the bondage of conviction ... [and] shattered faith in authority because he restored the authority of faith".[31] Afghānī, of course, provided some broad strokes, and actual reform – intellectual, social and legal – was to take place at the hands of Muhammad ʿAbduh, who can be said to have stood to Afghānī as St Simon stood to Condorcet, giving primacy to "social hygiene" over political power as the regulator of society.[32]

Such hygiene is to be had with the reform of religion, which, after all, Afghānī regarded as the backbone of social order.[33] And as Laroui has shown with customary perspicacity, this reformism – which he attributes entirely to Afghānī – is very much in the spirit of the Enlightenment. Of the fundamental motifs of classical Muslim reformism can be cited a utilitarianism in the conception of law, a naturalism in the conception of the world.[34] Indeed, the very core of the reformism is the repudiation of all authority that intervenes between the reformer and the origin to which reform is seen as a return: the Koran and the salutary example of early Islamic history. Islam, according to reformism, knows no authority save that of reason, and what passes for religious authority, such as the Caliphate and the various ecclesiastical offices, are nothing for ʿAbduh but secular offices which carry no doctrinal authority.[35] Nothing is authoritative but the pristine condition of Islam.

With historical Islam thus marginalized, ʿAbduh could embark on the reinterpretation of the Koran in the light of reason – the historical reason of the time: the fundamental criterion is contained in the notion that Islam is a religion of ease, tolerance and conformity with the conditions of human life, and is in this sense primeval, and thus the truest, historically the most versatile. Religions are subject to the laws of evolution, for the earliest of the true religions, with implicit reference to Judaism, is in conformity with the earlier stages of human history when right and wrong had to be arbitrarily dictated. A higher stage, implicitly with reference to Christianity, is clear when right and wrong are exhorted with reference to sentiment and to emotional arousal. Finally, with Islam, it is reason that is addressed.[36] Islam is thus transformed into a natural religion, and the reform of society is seen to reside in ridding it of the debris of history and revivifying the general sense of its original texts so they could have a contemporary relevance, in such a manner that Islamic law would become a particular variant of natural law. This reformed Islam is, incidentally, much in keeping with the laudatory ideas some Enlightenment thinkers held about Islam as a natural religion, superior to Christianity on this score, and in keeping with the natural course of social life.[37] After this naturalistic and utilitarian interpretation, little remains, in substantive terms, of Islam as it existed; what remains is a symbolic order.[38]

In the light of this legacy, it is hard to see what remained of Afghānī's irrationalist vitalism, which was the mainstay of his political theorizing and agitation, alongside his reformist notion of restoration. In historical terms, these two facets of his legacy have had separate careers, except to the mind of the Indian philosopher Sir Muhammad Iqbal (1876–1938). Iqbal combined German irrationalism and reformist naturalism and utilitarianism, after the fashion of Syed Ahmad Khan and the very similar efforts of Muhammad ʿAbduh, but he was of course working in a different tradition and circumstance to that experienced in modern Arab history.[39]

In fact, but for the possibilities inherent in the notion of reform as restoration, and therefore the implicit assumption of a subliminal historical continuity, which have been explored above, there is little in Islamic reformism of the Romantic politics of Afghānī. Reformist Islam has come to dominate official Islam, but until recently constituted only a subculture in the Arab World, where public life (with the exception of marginal and relatively backward areas like the Arabian Peninsula) has been dominated by nationalism, liberalism and various forms of socialism, and where the legal and educational systems, traditionally the mainstay of ecclesiastical authority, rapidly became secular.

What vitalist ideologies there were had an altogether different genealogy and had no reference to Afghānī. One would cite here some strands of Arab nationalism, such as the early doctrine of the Baʿth [Resurrection] Party now in power in Syria and Iraq. According to this doctrine, Arabism "does not indicate spatial properties and betrays no passage of time"; it is "the fount of theories, and is not born of thought but is wet-nurse of thought". The national self, the historical subject, is itself a criticism of pure intellection and a reaffirmation of life.[40] Similar notions, buttressed with detailed historical researches, can be found in the writings of theorists of the Syrian Social Nationalist Party of the 1940s, 50s, and 60s, and the advocates of infra-historical micro-nationalisms, such as Maronitism in Lebanon.

Contemporary Islamism, a recent phenomenon which dates in earnest only from the 1970s, adapted the vitalist elements in nationalism, the prevalent political and ideological culture in the Arab World, and took advantage of its versatility, which has already been mentioned, to assimilate vitalism to its own purposes. It can be said that Islamism insinuated itself, with a good measure of success, via a process of renaming of the subject, whose identity is constituted by vitalist associations, into the nationalist ideological sphere and coloured itself accordingly. In so doing, it has resurrected the Romanticism of Afghānī and re-established him as the fount of authenticity and its main proponent and, indeed, its idol.

Islamist political and cultural movements have taken over Afghānī's Romanticism with different pitches and emphases. A few have made a thorough reclamation of its abstract Jacobinism, a tendency which we can see in the most acute manifestations in Khomeinist tendencies. Others have seen in it almost a fact of nature, seeing in the indication of raw identities a matter instinctively apprehended by any mind attuned to the workings of nature – in this case, the nature of Muslims; an otherwise excellent history of modern Arabic thought has been written from this perspective.[41] Yet others have adapted this Romanticism as a cultural form of an essentially nationalist impulse. To this latter trend belong the hybrid tendencies which seek to translate various aspects of a modern political programme into Islamic terminology in order to authenticate and thus authorize them[42] or to develop an authentic "Islamic" method of social science whose metaphysical bearings are not Western, and which, not unnaturally, devolve to a restatement of some modern social science terms in a context where Islam acts as a myth of origin and charter of legislation, with an admixture of a vitalist epistemology.[43] In all these instances, Romantic Islamism is the name under which a hypernationalist cultural programme is officiated.

More directly relevant to the theme of this essay, however, is the reaction of universalist ideologies to the discourse on authenticity. The discourse of authenticity has rarely come into its own, outside Islamist circles, without being associated with some universalist discourse. Some illustrative examples drawn from the work of contemporary philosophers will suffice to show how this Romanticism was received and assimilated, although instances could be multiplied at will. Resistance to the notion of authenticity in the Arab World has been feeble in the recent past due to a number of manifest political circumstances, not the least of which being that the Arab World has not been immune from the worldwide resurgence of atavisim, ethnic and religious bigotry and fundamentalist religiosity.

One primary mechanism according to which linkages between universalism and particularist Romanticism are made is the simple act of naming that has already been encountered. The prominent philosopher, Professor Z.N. Mahmoud, a logical positivist by philosophical tendency and a liberal in politics, propounds a programme for the construction of an indigenous Arab philosophy starting from "the self". To this end, immediate apprehension is the epistemological key, for it is through introspection, he claims, that we can unveil the principles out of which arise "our" judgements on all matters. Such is his manner of seizing the authentic, which he finds in instances from the Arab past, from which he then derives his liberal principles of liberty and rationality. The combination assures the Arabs not only of the capacity for science, but also human dignity.[44]

Not all attempts have been as crude and awkward as this self-authentication by a very skilled technical philosopher. What Professor Mahmoud did was to bring into prominence – he has a vast readership – a number of staple ideas in Islamist circles since the time of Muhammad ʿAbduh: that revivalism is the axial mode of cultural and political discourse and authenticity the sole means of actual success as of moral probity; that as a result, historical practice is an act of authenticating desires or programmes for the present and the future; and that this authentication involves reference to past events still somehow alive at the core of the invariant historical subject, events which are repeatable, in the act of healing the breach between past and future. Thus parliamentary democracy is presented as a simple revalorization of the *shūra*, a process of consulting clan chiefs in early Islamic times, and rationality becomes a reclamation of the work of Averroes and of Ibn Khaldun, while freedom becomes a repetition of Muʾtazilite theological theses on free will, and socialism is made to stand in direct continuity with peasant rebellions of the tenth and eleventh centuries.

The past therefore becomes the paradigm of a present which must be authentic if it is to be in keeping with the *Volksgeist* and consequently merit serious cultural and political consideration. Past and future are unified by their substratum, the national essence, going beyond which is akin to breaking the laws of organic nature. It is this sense of historical continuity beyond history which has driven some Marxist philosophers to try to assimilate the discourse of authenticity. We can see this clearly in the monumental history of Arab-Islamic philosophy of Hussein Mroueh, assassinated not long ago. In it an attempt was made to separate two modalities of historical time, one of relevance today and the other redundant. The relevant one was, not unnaturally, "materialist tendencies" which might afford a point of linkage between past and future.[45] The past is liberated of its historicity and posited as the fount of desired continuities with a desired future, and the past is again cast in the future anterior, as if the spell of teleology is cast.

The same is discernible in the apologetic tenor of some of the most sophisticated Marxist writings on Arab-Islamic thought. As against the charge by some writers that time in classical Arabic thought is atomized by occasionalism, one scholar cites the notion of analogy current in Islamic legal theory as well as in theology. Rather than seeing in analogy the primacy of the key term – the precedent – he slants his analysis in the other direction and finds in the practice of analogy a reaffirmation of historicity rather than the denial of history which it in fact is, for it is an affirmation of only one time, a time of superlative ontological weight, the time of the text and precedent.[46] The same author also follows a long tradition in finding in Ibn Khaldun's metaphysical hierarchies a notion of class stratification, and discovers the Marxist theory of accumulation in the theological metaphors with which Ibn Khaldun formulates his discourse on economic activity.[47]

Thus is the anti-Enlightenment polemic interiorized in the bodies of philosophies whose fundamental motifs had been derived from the Enlightenment, and thus is a heritage invented by the elimination of history as past and its retrieval as a form of the present. There is no great secret by which one can explain the invasion by the trope of authenticity and its setting of assumptions that others feel constrained to adopt. But for the understanding of this we must leave the terrain of philosophy for that of society and polity.

Notes

1. See Abdallah Laroui, "The Arabs and Social Anthropology", in *The Crisis of the Arab Intellectual*, transl. Diarmid Cammell, Berkeley and Los Angeles 1976, pp. 44–80; and Aziz Al-Azmeh, "*Islamic Studies and the European Imagination*", Exeter 1986, this volume, ch. 7. For a close textual study of otherness in another historical context, see François Hartog, *Le Miroir d'Hérodote: Essai sur la représentation de l'autre*, Paris 1980.

2. The relation of Arabism and Islamism is exceedingly complex, and the reader is referred to the voluminous works of a conference on this matter: *Al Qawmīya al-ʿArabīyya wal-Islām* [*Arab Nationalism and Islam*], Beirut 1981. See Aziz Al-Azmeh, "Islamism and Arab Nationalism", *Review of Middle East Studies*, 4, 1988, pp. 33–51, this volume, ch. 3.

3. *An Islamic Response to Imperialism: Political and Religious Writings of Sayyid Jamal al-Din "al-Afghānī"*, transl. Nikki Keddie, Berkeley and Los Angeles, 1968. See also Homa Pakdaman, *Djamal-Ed-Din Assad Abadi dit Afghānī*, Paris 1969. On Syed Ahmad Khan, see Christian W. Troll, *Sayyid Ahmad Khan: A Reinterpretation of Muslim Theology*, New Delhi 1978.

4. A. Hourani, *Arabic Thought in the Liberal Age*, London 1962, is a most serviceable introduction to its topic in English. For a rigorous technical study, see Malcolm H. Kerr, *Islamic Reform: The Political and Legal Theories of Muhammad ʿAbduh and Rashid Rida*, Berkeley and Los Angeles 1966. It must be pointed out that studies on modern Arabic thought in English have achieved none of the seriousness of studies of comparable movements in India, of which one could mention V.C. Joshi, ed., *Rammohun Roy and the Process of Modernization in India*, New Delhi 1975; and Partha Chatterjee, *Nationalist Thought and the Colonial World*, London 1986. Fundamental for the study of modern Arab thought in a European language is Abdallah Laroui, *L'Idéologie arabe contemporaire*, Paris 1967.

5. See Taha Parla, *The Social and Political Thought of Ziya Gökalp*,

Leiden 1985; and William Cleveland, *The Making of an Arab Nationalist: Ottomanism and Arabism in the Life and Thought of Sati al-Husri*, Princeton 1971.

6. Şerif Mardin, *The Genesis of Young Ottoman Thought: A Study in the Modernization of Turkish Political Ideas*, Princeton 1962.

7. Cf. the approximate sketch of Abdessalam Bin Abdelālī, "Heidegger ḍidd Hegel" [Heidegger contra Hegel], *Dirāsāt ʿArabīyya*, 19, no. 4, 1983, pp. 93, 96.

8. Jamāl al-Dīn al-Afghānī, *Al-Aʿmāl al-Kāmila* [Complete works], ed. M. ʿUmāra, Cairo, n.d., pp. 130, 312–13; and *Al-ʿUrwa al-Wuthqā*, Cairo 1958, pp. 9–12 and passim.

9. Afghānī, *Al-Aʿmāl al-Kāmila*, p. 147, and *Al-Aʿmāl al-majhūla* [Unknown works], ed. Alī Shalash, London 1987, p. 78.

10. Afghānī, *Al-Aʿmāl al-majhūla*, pp. 80–81.

11. For instance, L. Gumplowicz, "Un sociologiste arabe du XIVe siècle", in *Aperçus sociologiques*, New York 1963, pp. 201–26 (originally published in 1898); *Geschichte der Staatstheorien*, Innsbruck 1905, par. 59; F. Oppenheimer, *System der Soziologie*, 2nd edn, Stuttgart 1964, vol. 2, pp. 173–4. See also Aziz Al-Azmeh, *Ibn Khaldun in Modern Scholarship*, London 1981, pp. 157 ff.

12. Afghānī, *Al-Aʿmāl-Kāmila*, pp. 443–4.

13. R.G. Collingwood, *The Idea of History*, Oxford 1946, p. 91.

14. Afghānī, *Al-Aʿmāl al-Kāmila*, p. 153.

15. Ibid., pp. 157–64.

16. *Al-ʿUrwa al-Wuthqā*, p. 20.

17. Gaston Bachelard, *Dialectique de la durée*, Paris 1950, p. 52.

18. Ḥasan Ḥanafī, *Dirāsāt falsafīyya* [Philosophical Studies], Cairo 1988, pp. 52–7.

19. Waḍḍāḥ Sharāra, *Ḥawla baʿḍ mushkilāt ad-dawla fil-mujtamaʿ wal-thaqāfa al-Arabiyyayan* [Some Problems Concerning the State in Arab Society and Culture], Beirut 1981, p. 71.

20. Quoted in Ernst Cassirer, *Philosophy of Symbolic Forms*, New Haven CT, 1955, vol. 2, p. 106.

21. *Al-ʿUrwa al-Wuthqā*, p. 20.

22. G.W.F. Hegel, *Phenomenology of the Spirit*, transl. A.V. Miller, Oxford 1977, pars 584, 590, 593.

23. G.W.F. Hegel, *Philosophy of Right*, transl. T.M. Knox, Oxford 1967, par. 4.

24. See the remarks on Dilthey in the excellent work of Stepan Odouev, *Par les sentiers de Zarathoustra: Influence de la pensée de Nietzsche sur la philosophie bourgeoise allemande*, transl. Catherine Emery, Moscow 1980, pp. 137–8.

25. Laroui, *L'Ideologie arabe contemporaire*, p. 66.

26. Afghānī, *Al-Aʿmāl al-majhūla*, p. 81.

27. Aziz Al-Azmeh, *Al-Turāth bayn al-Sulṭān wat-tārīkh* [Heritage: Power and History] Casablanca and Beirut 1987, pp. 91ff.

28. Cf. the analyses of Hedwig Konrad, *Étude sur la métaphore*, Paris 1939, p. 88; and Paul Ricoeur, *The Rule of Metaphor*, transl. R. Czerny et al., Toronto 1977, pp. 207–11.

29. Text in Keddie, transl., *An Islamic Response*, pp. 183, 187.

30. Ibid., p. 183.

31. Karl Marx, in Karl Marx and Frederick Engels, *Collected Works*, London 1975, vol. 3, p. 182.

32. Cf. Robert Wolker, "Saint-Simon and the Passage from Political to Social Science", in Anthony Pagden, ed., *The Languages of Political Theory in Early Modern Europe*, Cambridge 1987, pp. 335–6.

33. Afghānī, *Al-Aʿmāl al-Kāmila*, p. 130 and passim.

34. Abdallah Laroui, *Islam et modernité*, Paris 1987, pp. 134–47.

35. Muḥammad ʿAbduh, *Al-Aʿmāl al-Kāmila* [Complete works], ed. M. ʿUmāra, Beirut 1972, vol. 3, pp. 287, 289.

36. ʿAbduh, *Al-Aʿmāl al-Kāmila*, pp. 448–56.

37. ʿAbduh, *Al-Aʿmal al-Kāmila*, pp. 282–311; and Muḥammad Rashīd Riḍā, *Tārīkh al-ustādh al-Imām Muḥammad ʿAbduh* [Biography of Muhammad ʿAbduh], Cairo 1931, vol. 1, p. 614. In general, see the excellent study of Kerr, *Islamic Reform.*

38. Laroui, *Islam et modernité*, pp. 127–30.

39. Muhammad Iqbal, *The Reconstruction of Religious Thought in Islam*, London 1934, pp. 4–15, 42–55, 126–31, 148–54, 165–9.

40. Michel Aflaq, *Fī Sabīl al-Baʿth* [For the Baath], Beirut 1958, pp. 43, 44, 158.

41. Muḥammad Jābir al-Anṣārī, *Taḥawwulāt al-fikr was-siyāsa fil-sharq al-ʿArabī, 1930–1970* [Transformations of Thought and Politics in the Arab East, 1930–1970], Kuwait 1980.

42. For instance, Ḥanafī, *Dirāsāt falsafiyya*; and *Al-Turāth wal-tajdīd* [Heritage and Renewal], Beirut 1981; and cf. Aziz Al-Azmeh, *Al-Turāth*, pp. 164–8.

43. For instance, ʿAdil Ḥusain, *Naḥwa fikr ʿarabī jadīd: an-nāṣiriyya wal-tanmiya wal-dimuqrāṭiyya* [Towards a New Arab Thought: Nasserism, Development and Democracy], Cairo 1985.

44. Zakī Najīb Mahmūd, *Tajdīd al-fikr ʿal-arabī* [The Renewal of Arabic Thought], Beirut 1980, pp. 274, 283.

45. Ḥusain Muruwwa, *Al-Nazaʿāt al-māddīyya fil-falsafa al-ʿarabiyya al-islāmīyya* [Materialist Trends in Arab-Islamic Philosophy], Beirut 1978, 3 volumes.

46. Mahmūd Amīn al-ʿĀlim, "Mafhūm al-zamān fil-fikr al-ʿarabī al-islāmī" [The Conception of Time in Arab-Islamic Thought], in *Dirāsāt fil-Islām*, Beirut 1980, pp. 110–11. See Aziz Al-Azmeh, "Islamic Legal Theory and the Appropriation of Reality", in Aziz Al-Azmeh, ed., *Islamic Law: Social and Historical Contexts*, London 1988, pp. 250–65.

47. Mahmūd Amīn al-ʿĀlim, "Muqaddimat Ibn Khaldūn – Madkhal ibistimulūjī" [Ibn Khaldun's Muqaddima: An Epistemological Introduction], in *Al-Fikr al-ʿArabī*, Beirut 1978, vol. 6, pp. 37, 41–2, 45–6.

3

Arab Nationalism and Islamism

Like other religions, Islam is not a generic essence, but a nominal entity that conjoins, by means of a name, a variety of societies, cultures, histories and polities. Some hagiolatrous (or worse) varieties of Islam in India, for instance, are no closer to Islam "in essence" than certain contemporary African messianic prophetisms are to Christianity, though the "Hinduism" of the former does not, except in specific fundamentalist moments, alter its title to Islamism. If religion is a determinate concept denoting the elaboration of belief, practice, society, polity and the world in general by means of the opposition between the sacred and the profane, a particular religion, as a generic phenomenon, adds virtually nothing to this save a name and a number of associated classificatory tokens (basic dogmas and fundamental devotions and, above all, specific textual and other genealogies). The determinate existence of a religion is always historical, the specific production and circulation of what has been termed *les biens religieux*[1] in a specific social location by and for specific groups involved in the social and political dialectic, A religion is always produced and reproduced according to the exigencies of society and polity, though this is almost invariably undertaken in terms of a fundamentalist motif, a myth of origin claiming a particular textual genealogy.

This marriage of fundamental heterogeneity and fundamentalist homogenization, and the claims of the latter to primacy, is the first cautionary point I wish to make before the connections of Islamism and Arab nationalism are explored. Given the assumption that there is little that is generically Islamic about Islam, the relation between contemporary Islamic movements and ideologies and Arab nationalism is not one which finds its bearings in a comparative juxtaposition of Islam and Arab nationalism, which charts their concordance and discordance or which registers the correspondence or conflict of identities, as in the standard positions on the matter.[2] But this should not imply that there is not something generically religious about Islam and whatever classifies itself as Islamic, for these call forth immediately and valorize the vast repertoire of tokens and images that have been associated with that constellation of specific cadences of the relation between the sacred and the profane that history and collective memory have registered as Islamic. The positive connection between Islam and Arab nationalism takes place, in terms of the first, on the domain of sacralization, and in terms of the second, on that of Arabization. They relate, not as pre-existent *sui generis* entities, but as they are separately or jointly generated in terms of antecedent (and ever-changing) ideological, sociological, political and cultural locations.

Like things sacred, nations and their ideological components are constantly fashioned and refashioned. They do not belong to the realm of nature, and are no more the results of a seminal continuity and fixity than religious communities, but are rather delimited as political units by nationalist movements, and thus can not be said to antedate them except in the fantastic genealogies of nationalism.[3] That nationalism, including Arab nationalism, is not generically coterminous with the existence of the Arabs is the second cautionary point I wish to make; whereas Lebanese Nasserism and that of the Syrians, for instance, share the same political language, their socio-political and cultural import is utterly distinct, as distinct perhaps as the Baathism of Tripoli and of South Lebanon, or as Beirut Nasserism of 1975 and 1984, especially with a view to relation with Islamism.

This seemingly enigmatic situation is indicated in order to underline two matters of relevance to the relation between Islamism and Arab nationalism. Chief among these is that nationalism, like Islam, is sociologically indeterminate,[4] in the sense that the politico-cultural unity it espouses, and the politico-cultural unification whose agency it is, are not ones which can be exclusively apportioned to a particular class or coalition of classes, not even the "middle class". Put in another way, this indicates that the different parties to the social and political dialectic (classes or political groups of a more various bearing, as would be more appropriate, in the case of Arab and other Third World nationalisms) can be said to constitute distinct types of the same nationalism, types which have in common a unitary political vocabulary but different political, social and other programmes, programmes which may be in fact antagonistic.

It is in the pores of this common ground of social and political indeterminancy that the relation between Arab nationalism and Islamism is located. A connection at the level of purely semiotic function seems the only one possible in the case of two such utterly different substances as Arab nationalism and Islamism, the former being an ideology, a set of normative enunciations whose primary bearing is political and cultural, and the latter a religion which only recently carved for itself an ideological and political space distinct from nationalism, alongside its religious and associated civil spheres (a matter which will be addressed later). This semiotic connection can be seen to have been borne out by, among other things, such morsels of empirical evidence as are available on the composition of political crowds in Arab countries[5] which show, in the case of Syria for instance, that the Islamic and the Nasserist crowds of the 1960s were virtually indistinguishable.[6] Similarly, the same social groups in Cairo, with slight differences concerning rural affiliations, account for the cadres of left-wing as well as the most radical of Islamic groups such as the famous *Takfīr* and *Taḥrīr*;[7] and the same urban petty trading elements in Syria gave Nasser much of his public strength as today nourishes the Muslim Brothers.[8]

But this does not imply some protean oriental essence so permeating Arab nationalism and Islamism as to make them two avatars of one. Neither does it imply a fundamental concordance, nor again simply the parasitic use of one by the other. After all, the same sociological community between the Muslim Brothers and the Nasserists extends to the constituency of the Communist Party, a fact which must account, at least in part, for the particular fractiousness of the conflict between these various parties.[9] What this political and ideological indeterminancy does imply is that a particularly tenacious urban constituency has weathered the vagaries of colonialist and imperialist depredation, and has sought to articulate its position in a variety of manners consonant with the political transformations of the various Arab countries, with specific configurations within the political and social dialectic and language. What this implies, further, is that rather than Arab nationalism or Islamism politically and ideologically "representing" this particular social group, this social group finds its bearings in the context of the polity at large. It does this not simply because it coheres economically (as petty production and trading) and has proved resistant to the economic disarticulation of the various countries in the course of development (though this resistance, in some countries such as Syria, is crumbling), but more importantly, because it coheres socially in terms of a patrimonial mode of organization. Indeed, not cohering politically for any length of time, this group appears to be seeking social retrenchment in terms of Islam today precisely because it has lost its political cover with the waning of the old patrician classes within the boundaries of which the political instance was located, and the construction of states on the basis of differently constituted polities. Bereft of its political instance due to political revolution, the civil society of the cities and of the transplanted villages was exposed to direct political direction and unaccounted for by the social structure, and thus resorted to a social involution recorded in the type of programme espoused today by Islamic political movements.

What are now rather anachronistic trenches of civil society, the values connected with Arabic commercial urban life and their correlative social structures, were previously not defensive devices but the very fabric of society. When they were still firmly articulated in the context of the society and polity at large, they were mobilized and drafted into the nationalist cause of the nationalist sections of the patrimonial notability, such as that organized by the Wafd in Egypt, the National and People's Parties of Syria, or the Makhzan-related movements of Morocco, in the (officially or unofficially) colonial period. They were simultaneously mobilized by means of a leadership enjoying an ample, albeit immediately perceptible and measurable, social distance from them by specifically Islamist movements, often organized in the context of local philanthropic societies, some of the best known of which included the *Maqasid* of Beirut and *Jamʿīyyat at-tamaddun al-islāmī* of Damascus – the latter was particularly important in the emergence of the Muslim Brothers.[10] Before the emergence of formal political and social associations such as the nationalist and Islamist organizations (of which some examples have just been cited), the politics of the social mass were concerned with particular issues and took the form of local riots in response to immediate issues such as rises in prices, the appointment of particularly covetous and avaricious officials, or extortionate taxation.[11] And before the emergence of such formal organizations towards the end of the nineteenth century, there does not seem to have been a consistent ideology, or ideological motif, on the basis of which mobilization was undertaken. Popular colloquial poems concerning the 1839 riots in Damascus, for instance, contain neither religious nor nationalist motifs, but extol the virtues of rioting toughs after the manner of the popular tales of ʿAntar and Abū Zaid al-Hilālī,[12] whereas the near-riotous popular processions of Damascus retained, well into the present century, the character of festivals where local excellence, especially of manliness and *futuwwa*, were the main spectacles.[13]

Whether anti-European riots, such as those of Cairo under Napoleonic occupation or, more mediately, the massacre of Christians in Damascus in 1860, or even the activities of the Muslim Brothers in Palestine in the 1940s or the Cairene riots of 1977, should or should not be considered proto-nationalist is therefore as moot a point as the question of whether ʿAbd al-Qādir's resistance to the French in Algeria or other activities associated with mysticism and Mahdism are proto-nationalist. Not all opposition to foreigners is by nature nationalist, as nothing is nationalist by nature, nor is nationalism a necessary and most perfect stage in an inexorable evolutionary scheme, as seems for long to have been the axial assumption in much of evolutionist and development theory, an assumption spelt out with customary succinctness by Marcel Mauss in the proposition that nations are the most perfect form of life in society.[14] Such religious opposition to the perfidies of foreign power and subjugation almost invariably remained resolutely local, and if they became components in nationalist coalition, they became so almost by misadventure, as with the Sanūsiyya, and were at best para-nationalist.

What was proto-nationalist, however, and partook of the hegemonic politico-cultural programme of nationalism and thus gained a certain political coherence, was the *salafīyya* in countries of the Maghreb. This has been argued for Algeria, on the assumption that one need not have been overtly nationalistic in order to be proto-nationalist.[15] This seems to be true in so far as the *salafīyya* deliberately worked towards the elimination of particularistic religious rusticity as was embodied in the maraboutic movements,[16] tainted as they were with colonialist collaborationism. In Morocco, similarly, it is possible to speak of a proto-nationalist salafism which was all the more difficult to disentangle from nationalism proper as the two were articulated in the overall leadership of sultanic Makhzan system.[17]

This practical, operational indistinctness should not, however, be allowed to obscure the distinction which is more clearly marked in the Mashriq. In effect, the nationalism of important sections of the Maghribi national movements is closer in political language and symbolism to the "nationalism" of the Muslim Brothers than to Arab nationalism properly speaking – ʿAllāl al-Fāsī provides a good example of this. In the constitutive phase of Arab nationalism, the enemy was the Turk, not the Infidel,[18] and it will be remembered that the caliphal motif was represented by Kawākibī not as a change of political system, but for the accession of an Arab to the caliphal office – an idea more extant until the 1950s than has been supposed, and one which seems to account for much of the wider political ambitions of Kings Abdullah and Ibn Saud, and for not a little of their extensive pan-Arab connections. Pre-*salafīyya* reformism exemplified by Muhammad ʿAbduh was a separate movement; the public career of ʿAbduh himself was not exactly evidence of exemplary nationalism, and the *salafīyya* of Rashīd Riḍā did not, likewise, arrogate to itself a directly political role except with so many reservations as to render effectively defunct the idea of Islam as the prime title of political community.[19] Alongside it was nationalism, to which the field was left.

Politics, as before, was the preserve of the notability which accounted for nationalism, while *salafīyya* reformism engaged in theorizing the reconstitution of civil society in terms of itself rather than in terms of politics. In the colonial period, the *salafīyya* project was directed at the solidification of civil society in the face, not directly of political domination, but mediately, in opposition to nefarious foreign influence ("cultural colonialism", the counter-Crusading motif, and so on), by means of a communalism which, in preparation for active combat, sought, like nationalism, to eradicate civil differences within society and integrate it in the communalist instance.[20] In this sense, the community is substituted for the nation, and the boundaries of the community become the physical and social boundaries of polity:[21] thus are excluded from the bounds of polity the majority of the population, which was still rustic, as well as all elements of the population that do not belong to the community of believers which, almost by the force of nature, always received what in effect was a local definition. The one instance of greater catholicity was born of the very different circumstances of an expanding polity supported by the *salafī* creed of Wahhabism. Itself the polity – a culture being imposed on the body of nature that was civil society – it was unencumbered, unlike the wider Arab context where politics resided in the natural body of a nationalist notability. This Wahhabism could attempt to forge a society rid of all unevenness and made uniform by means of breaking and eliminating particularity and reconstituting the atomized mass by means of Wahhabism.[22] Thus, paradoxically, the anti-nationalist Wahhabi movement in fact attempted to fulfil a historical function normally associated with nationalism.

Wahhabism is the sort of para-nationalism that lies at the limit of that which is possible for *salafīyya* politics. There is an almost radically anti-political impulse in all salafism, one which regards politics as an incidental activity in a world defined in terms of civil society, or regulations concerning moral–religious proprieties. That is why *salafī* movements, albeit part of many a nationalist coalition, are profoundly inimical to nationalism, especially the nationalism of the inter-war period which was, in essence, political, without much of the ideological armoury of the 1940s and later – a lack which, in the case of Egypt, for instance, made Egyptianism (and I exclude Pharaonism and Mediterraneanist occidentalism), defined in general nationalist terms not specifically in contrast to Arabism, and rendered it possible for Egyptianism to join up with Arabism and for the two to shade off into one another according to conjunctural exigencies.

This shading of one nationalism into a wider one takes place according to very much the same mechanism as those which, ideologically, connect Islamism and Arab nationalism. In essence, Arab nationalism may have been utterly unconnected with Islam. Islam plays no role whatsoever in the ideology of the Arab Nationalist Movement, and there is far more to this than the fact that its historical leadership included a Christian (George Ḥabash) – Baathism was founded by another Christian, but the attitude there was different. A most prominent exponent of Arab nationalist ideology, Saṭi ʿal-Ḥuṣri, who had been schooled under the Ottoman Empire, while stating that Islam was one moment of Arab nationalism, defined Arab nationalism in contrast to Islamism and to colonialism in one and the same breath, proceeding to give Arabism a linguistic definition,[23] and not omitting to castigate Muslim ecclesiastics for their opposition to Arab nationalism.[24] Another prominent Arab nationalist, ʿAbd al-Laṭīf Sharāra, insisted, like many school textbooks do today in Syria and Iraq, that Arabism antedates Islam by far, and that the Akkadians and Phoenicians were Arabs.[25] Another prominent nationalist, one of the original impulses of Baathism, saw the matter (as Huṣri also did) in Comtean terms, and regarded the Middle Ages as a religious age which is superseded by the age of nationalities.[26]

The connection with Islam is not intrinsic or conceptual, but associative, and is only retrospectively theorized. For ʿAflaq, the relation of Muhammad to Arabism is very much akin to that of microcosm and macrocosm; it is Arabism itself which is endowed with the potential of spirit to transcend matter, for Islam is but one moment within Arabism,[27] and it is to the status of Arabism, which transcends mere politics, that the degraded Islam of the day is to be lifted.[28] It is Arabism which is the main discursive term, and Islam is coopted as at best a privileged adjunct, not as a self-sustaining unit. A recent semantic and content analysis of Nasser's speeches has shown that, contrary to a habitual misconception, a sharp separation between Arabism and Islam is made almost from the very beginning, and the relation between the two is construed as one of co-operation and mutual support, not of integration.[29]

The peripheral discursive role of Islam in nationalist ideology appears to be a transposition into the body of discourse of an actual power relation between nationalist polity and the Islamic constituency which radical nationalist politicians took "the people" to be. The contrast with the earlier patrician nationalists, for whom "the people" were no other than their very own political and social clients, varies in its starkness, but is almost always arresting. In both cases we see at work matters indicated earlier, the civic orientation of Islamism and the political being of Arabism, hence its practical ascendancy and its power to patronize the former. Though Arab nationalist ideology and discourse never bore Islamist ideas (it is well to remember that the Nasserist constitution of 1958 made no mention of Islam, as was later to become *de rigeur*), Islamic input beamed at "the people" under nationalist auspices was laden with Arabism – school textbooks for instance,[30] or Friday sermons,[31] or the Islamic socialism of various regimes and times and its impact on Muslim Brother conceptions (especially with Musṭafā al-Sibāʿi and Muḥammad al-Ghazālī), not to speak of the Azhar-related institutions set up under Nasser or the equivalent but much more restricted institutions set up by the Syrian Baath.

Arab nationalism coopted Islam, but did not engage it. So long as Islamic thought and activity were not directly in opposition to the nationalistic regimes, they were left largely on their own, albeit not autonomous (it was not until the days of Sadat in 1979 that an attempt was made to take over the 5,000-odd Egyptian mosques independent of the Awqaf ministry). This cooptation of Islam, while it was undertaken in the name of Arabism and metamorphosed according to the particular physiognomies of Arabism, still left it unintegrated, an independent though not self-sufficient auxiliary. There was also a high density of references to things Islamic, and this brought into play an extremely important rhetorical (in the neutral sense) mechanism which as been encountered with regional and Arab nationalism: relations of metaphor and metonymy between Arabism and Islam. It is by rhetorical means such as these that the same statement can be made to refer to both, or an object made to belong to both, or to move from one to the other. For in reality they are unintegrated, separate, autonomous spheres, the one (Arabism) political, and the other (Islam) more germane to a particular urban or recently urbanized civil society. Polity was seen, under radical nationalism, politically to represent rather than naturally to lead, as had been the case with patrician nationalist regimes.

Once released, tokens of Arabism or Islamism automatically call forth a host of others, many of which are mutually translatable. Thus the constant recourse to the battle of Qādasīyya in present-day Iraqi war propaganda interpellates both Arabic and Islamic echoes, and the constant dubbing of Iranian forces as “hordes of the Magians” is again one that calls forth symbols of Arabism (as against Persians) and of Islamism (as against Zoroastrianism). The shading of Arabism and Islamism into each other is accomplished by stripping both of their conceptual and political accoutrements, and utilizing them at the level of imagery as mute symbols, as tokens which suggest, by virtue of their tonality alone, a sphere of normative rectitude, and indeed contain the entirety of the issue within the rectitude of the word – Islam, Arabism, Qādasīyya. This is not an exercise in the obfuscation of issues but a natural political mystification, an ideological mobilization of the most elementary and visceral type, one that finds its most perfect analogue in the manner by which football fanatics are mobilized by recourse to a name they invest with normative rectitude, and as Roman and Byzantine circus factions were mobilized by the evocation of a colour. But though mute, such mobilization by means of images drawn from the symbolic sediments of the ages is always, deliberately or inadvertently, not equally open for all to respond. Specific shades of a mobilizing utterance simultaneously draw out different crowds, but do not necessarily reconstitute the social mass of the crowd into a uniform political direction.[32]

It is, I think, clear that much of this has to do with the political and civil constituency which radical nationalist regimes were (and are) attempting to construct. Whereas traditional nationalists appealed to a well-defined and inherited civil constituency, radical nationalist charismatic leaderships (a person in Egypt, a party in Syria, and so on) felt that charisma alone was insufficient. Being political leaderships of a fundamentally political and ideological constitution, and faced with civil constituencies whose "natural" leaderships, the traditional nationalists, were removed (eradicated in Syria, metamorphosed in Egypt), the new leadership sought to develop a political language which could take in "the people", now a cluster of civil communities under immense disarticulating pressures from the economy. Instead of the network of cousins and friends of friends which had been the previous *modus operandi* of polity, and before new such networks were set up and consolidated by the new incumbents of state power, the radical nationalist regimes adopted what has been aptly called "a sort of *koine* that Nasserism in particular favoured and diffused *mezzo voce* as a counterpoint, so to speak, to its Arabism and Arab socialism".[33] This entailed the adoption and reproduction of images and utterances of Islamic association, selected and constantly replenished from the symbolic repertoire of Arabic and Islamic history, images and utterances of great historical density, born of daily recall in the educational and religious systems. But the discourse in which things Islamic were evoked was modernist, not fundamentalist: it is the present that is contained in the past, not the reverse, though it does not exclusively consist of it. This modernist eclecticism was all pervasive. A theoretician of the Lebanese Communist Party, no doubt conjuring up and then appealing to "the people", even discovered in the Koran not only the Dialectics of Nature, but also the principles of cybernetics.[34]

Be that as it may, a number of conceptual features common to the ideologies of Arabism and Islamism rendered possible the association between them and their occasional power of mutual convertibility. Chief amongst these is what, in the circumstances, is an unfortunate homonymy: the word *umma* denotes the nationalist conception of the nation, as well as the Islamic community which would necessarily denote, for "the people", the civil community which binds their social universe. Another important feature is the ideal of social unity[35] and the correlative rejection of the notion of classes, a transhistorical unity subject to a historical alternance, to the alternation of periods of national autonomy or of religious rectitude with periods of foreign rule, of ungodliness, of decadence (*jāhiliyya*, *mulk*, *ṭāghūt*, *isti mār*, *inḥiṭāṭ*, and so on). Both the nationalist and the Islamist programmes espouse what in the not too dissimilar ideological condition of populism was described as a "primitivism", the restoration of a pre-colonial or caliphal utopia, the defenestration of the burden of history, the elision of change undergone as a result of all that which is inauthentic.[36] This restoration, of course, takes place at the expense and in spite of history, and is really more of an ontological than a temporal process. The Nation, or Islam, is the only positive element in a normative ideological system of which it itself is the sole criterion of rectitude and the exclusive axis of reference. The *umma*, Arab or Islamic, is the normative terminus of its ideological utterances and the images these utterances contain and interpellate. The ultimate triumph of rectitude, the restoration of primitive innocence, in both cases takes place by forces which are ultimately over and above history: the will in the case of nationalism and divine guidance in the case of Islamism – although it must be stressed that the more elaborate ideological discourse of nationalism adopted an evolutionist perspective which, in both its social-Darwinist (in the Arab Nationalist Movement or early Baathist writing) and Marxist (for instance the so-called neo-Baath and the Democratic Popular Front for the Liberation of Palestine) versions, was almost predestinarian.

The windfall, after the degeneration of radical nationalist regimes set in with internal and external failures, was very much to the advantage of Islamism. It was not difficult to make the transition between, say, the view on the Crusades held by nationalists and that held by Islamists. To the standard contention of nationalist historiography (oft repeated by Nasser) that the Crusades were an early manifestation of colonialism, Sayyid Quṭb simply said that it was in fact colonialism which was a camouflaged form of the Crusading spirit[37] without devaluing the normative weight of either term. The very repetition of Islamist images, alongside and within nationalism, was sufficient for the forging of an Islamist programme, for such a programme is made not of policies but of tokenist precepts. Clearly, the Caliphate, the declaration of present states as *dār al-ḥarb* after the manner of present-day Qutbists (following Maudūdī and Ibn ʿAbd al-Wahhāb), are Romantic political arguments rather than programmes; whatever actual programmes as related to political realities, such as the call for parliamentary democracy or for socialism, are an adjunct to the utopian motif, and hence appear as a call for *shūra* and *ʿadāla* respectively. The act of renaming is the act of ideologizing, of insertion within a particular world of images which call forth one another, but more importantly call forth particular social groups into the fray, almost by suggestion, because naming interpellates divisions between groups that adhere to a particular system of nomenclature and groups that do not legitimately belong to it, and are therefore outside and against it. The manifest everyday programme of Islamism is social and ethical in the first place, a sort of local reformism of morals carried away with universalist utopian aspirations. Right from the start, from the days of Afghānī and ʾAbduh, the strength of nations was seen to reside not only in unity but in moral rectitude[38] – uplifting the nation is undertaken not by means of education but by the return to the moral roots of strength.[39] This theme of authenticity and the retrieval of innocence has been the backbone of Islamism, and authenticity is practically seen to reside in the resuscitation of a social order built on a number of civil and moral principles which are seen rhetorically (that is, metonymically) to represent and fully to encompass the rest: issues concerned with the position of women, prohibition of alcoholic beverages and the like. That is why Islamic states are credibly declared established once any number, no matter how small, of these matters are legislated.[40] And that is why extremist Islamic organizations subject their membership to a thorough resocialization.[41]

Islamism became a political ideology, rather than just the sanctimonious philanthropism it had been (and still is for the majority) when it adapted nationalism. By this I mean that the centre of gravity of the homonymy and mutual convertibility of themes and symbols treated earlier shifted to the advantage of

Islamism: underdevelopment and imperialism became "cultural invasion", the Third World became "The Islamic World", liberation and independence became "Cultural Authenticity" (*aṣāla*). Most of these notions were conjured in the context of the Faisal–Nasser conflict of the 1960s, and the main source of finance for the authenticity industry remains Saudi Arabia and the Gulf States, which is not a negligible fact given media outlets of great appeal controlled by Arabian interests, not to speak of hundreds of thousands of Arabs who live in the Gulf States. One of the most unfortunate and harmful consequences of this spectacle is the hypernationalism of a number of former Marxists, especially in Egypt and in Lebanon, that has taken the form of a consistent and thorough advocacy of this concept of *aṣāla* at the expense of an appreciation of conjunctural and historical realities. In cases where such intellectuals are not now directly apologizing for movements such as the Muslim Brothers, this reification of Islam/Arabdom versus a demonology of the West on the part of true radicals can find no bearing in political reality except that which, willy-nilly, plays into the hands of Islamist politics.[42]

The adaptation of nationalism, admittedly in a very poor man's version of it, just as much as nationalism was a poor man's Hegelianism, was made possible by the degeneration of nationalist regimes. Islamism as a political ideology is not some ersatz nationalism, but the attempt of moribund social structures to perpetuate themselves in spite of and as against nationalist regimes under the aegis of which they first lost their patrimonial leadership and hence their political cover which shielded them as much as possible from the vagaries of development, and then lost their economic position through progressive declassment and relative pauperization. In addition, radical nationalist regimes, through political and professional organizations and agencies which are more means of direct penetration and control than means of popular mobilization, initially used direct political and administrative methods rather than clientilist avenues to control the body social. But this did not entail an attempt to fashion a body politic, for despotic regimes prefer an abstract "people" and a society as drained of politics as it is bereft of divisions. The fact, however, was and still is that Arab societies today exist in a state not only of social but also of temporal Balkanization, in which different social groups, regions, economic sectors and cultural patterns are changing at differential rates more related to outside pressures than to the mechanisms of an articulated whole, so that the state emerges as the vertical hinge of a geo-political entity which is otherwise disarticulated. In such circumstances, politics (nationalist politics) becomes direct administrative intervention, not the art of leading through hegemonic assent. The state itself, again, becomes the embodiment of a civil group (as the situation in Syria and Iraq and, much more mediately, in Egypt) whose *modus operandi* is civil, based on a network of cousins and friends of friends, albeit in the name of the nation.

In the circumstances it is hardly surprising that civil society, embattled and defunct but without perspective or hope, should seek to assert itself in civil terms as against the civil terms in the context of which the state operates[43] – the state, *dawla*, almost in the etymological sense of a patrimony, pertaining to someone and run by corps, not unlike modern analogues of Mamluks. It is not surprising that civil society, structurally moribund but closed, should protest against the reality of its folkloristic status by recourse to savage myths of origin. Finally, it is not surprising that such protest being closed to history, and its perspectives absent, they should, as Algerian traditionalism was aptly described, produce resistances rather than demands,[44] and that, consequently, one response of the state should be repression, one extreme limit of which was perhaps the suppression of the civil insurrection in Hama in January–February 1982.[45] The situation clearly involves a kind of social irredentism, and one which is articulated in terms of opposition to a godless order (for religion is impossible without an antithetical relation), by what takes itself for a cultural minority, albeit a social "majority". The result is that fundamentalist, that is, primitivist, Islamism acts as if it were a subaltern nationalism seeking a pre-nationalist paradise, and such could only be conceived in terms of images of an immediate civil past: a cosy world of cousins and secluded women, with its attendant security. The comparison with some subaltern European nationalisms comes to mind, as does the positing of fascist corporatism and organicism as the paradigm of such nationalisms[46] and the comparable para-nationalist Islamism of the Arab world today. This involution is not confined to the Sunni middle classes of Arab cities, but can also be seen to be manifested by other locations of Balkanization, in the paltry Christo-fascism of the Kaslik University, in the ideological space of which the Phalangist Party solicits its sustenance and elsewhere where communalist polity is under cultivation, sometimes in the most bizarre fashion.

Notes

1. P. Bourdieu, "Genèse et structure du champ religieux", *Revue Française de Sociologie*, 12, 1971. The nominalist definition of contemporary Islam was put forward in my *Al-Turāth bayn al-sulṭān waʾl-tārīkh*, Casablanca and Beirut 1987, pp. 51ff.

2. The most compendious register of these views in their different shades and orientations is the voluminous *Al-Qawmīya al-ʿarabiya wal-Islām* [Arab Nationalism and Islam], Beirut 1981.

3. See E. Gellner, *Nations and Nationalism*, Oxford 1983, ch. 5.

4. The corollary is, as S. Zubaida has suggested ("Theories of Nationalism", in G. Littlejohn et al., eds, *Power and the State*, London 1978), that there can be no sociology of nationalism in general, nor is nationalism the unitary object of sociological investigation.

5. There is, to my knowledge, regrettably no equivalent for Arab countries of E. Abrahamian's excellent article, "The Crowd in Iranian Politics, 1905–1953", *Past and Present*, 41, 1968.

6. R.A. Hinnesbusch, "The Islamic Movement in Syria: Sectarian Conflict and Urban Rebellion in an Authoritatarian-Populist Regime", in A.E. Hillal Dessouki, ed., *Islamic Resurgence in the Arab World*, New York 1982, p. 154.

7. S.E. Ibrahim, "Anatomy of Egypt's Militant Islamic Groups: Methodological Note and Preliminary Findings", *International Journal of Middle East Studies*, 12, 1980, p. 447.

8. H. Batatu, "Syria's Muslim Brethren", *MERIP Reports*, 12/9, 1982, p. 18; and cf. J. Reissner, *Ideologie und Politik der Muslimbrüder Syriens: Von den Wahlen 1947 bis zum Verbot unter as-Sisakli 1952*, Freiburg-im-Breisgau 1980.

9. Reissner, *Ideologie und Politik*, pp. 198–9.

10. For instance Reissner, *Ideologie und Politik*, pp. 86ff, 127–8.

11. For instance A. Raymond, "Quartiers et mouvements populaires au Caire au XVIIIe siècle", in P.M. Holt, ed., *Political and Social Change in Modern Egypt*, London 1968.

12. *Majmūʿat azjāl wa māwāwīl*, Zahiriyya Library, Manuscript no. 8749, fols 39–46 (now in the Assad National Library).

13. J. Lecerf and R. Tresse, "Les ʿArada de Damas", *Bulletin des Etudes Orientales*, 7–8, 1937–8.

14. "The Problem of Nationality", *Proceedings of the Aristotelian Society*, NS, 20, 1919–1920, pp. 242–3.

15. E. Gellner, *Muslim Society*, Cambridge 1981, p. 161.

16. Ibid., p. 166.

17. See A. Laroui, *Les Origines sociales et culturelles du nationalism marocain (1830–1912)*, Paris 1977, pp. 424ff.

18. The emergence of anti-Ottomanist Arabism is well traced in one case by P. Khoury who, however, adopts easy explanations rather too readily (*Urban Notables and Arab Nationalism: The Politics of Damascus, 1860–1920*, Cambridge 1983.

19. See H. Enayat, *Modern Islamic Political Thought*, London 1982, p. 76; and the subtle treatment of technical matters by Malcolm Kerr, *Islamic Reform*, Berkeley and Los Angeles 1966, ch. 5.

20. This statement was suggested by an inverse situation in which G. Balandier ("Messianismes et nationalismes en Afrique noire", *Cah. Int. de Sociologie*, 14, 1953, p. 63) contrasted Mahdist and Christian messianism in Black Africa.

21. Cf. R. Dumont, "Nationalism and Communalism", in *Religion/ Politics and History in India*, Paris and The Hague 1970, pp. 90–91.

22. See A. Al-Azmeh, "Wahhabite Polity", this volume ch. 6; and W. Sharāra, *Al-Ahl wal-ghanīma. Muqawwimāt as-siyāsa fil-Mamlaka al-ʿArabīya as-Suʾūdīya* [Clansmen and Booty: the Pillars of Politics in the Kingdom of Saudi Arabia], Beirut 1981.

23. *Mā-hiya al-qawmīyya?* [What is Nationalism?], 2nd edn, Beirut 1963, pp. 193, 257.

24. Ibid., p. 208.

25. *Al-Jānib ath-thaqāfī min al-qawmiyya al-ʿarabīyya* [Cultural Aspects of Arab Nationalism], Beirut 1961, pp. 38ff.

26. Z. Arsūzī, *Mashākilunā al-qawmīya wa mawqif al-aḥzāb minhā* [Our National Problems and Party-Political Positions towards them], Damascus 1956, p. 17.

27. *Fī sabīl al-Baʿth* [For the Baath], Beirut 1959, pp. 52–4.

28. Ibid., pp. 60, 91.

29. M. Nasr, *Al-Taṣawwur al-qawmī al-ʿarabī fī fikr Jamāl ʿAbd an-Nāṣir* [The Arab Nationalist Conception in Nasser's Thought], Beirut 1981, pp. 344ff, 360ff. O. Carré (*Les Frères Musulmans, 1928–1982*, Paris 1983, pp. 47ff) attributes to Nasser political conceptions of the Muslim Brothers.

30. Some of these were well studied by O. Carré, *La legitimation islamique des socialismes arabes. Analyse conceptuelle combinatoire des manuels scolaires egyptiens, syriens, et iraqiens*, Paris 1979.

31. See the informative but not very instructive dissertation of B.M. Borthwick, "The Islamic Sermon as a Channel of Political Communication in Syria, Jordan and Egypt", University of Michigan, Ann Arbor, 1965.

32. I examined these issues in my *Al-Turāth*, pp. 83ff.

33. O. Carré, "The Future for Gulf/Europe/America Relationship: A European View", in B.R. Pridham, ed., *The Arab Gulf and the West*, 1985, p. 238.

34. M. ʿItānī, *Al-Qurʾān fi ḍawʾ al-fikr al-māddi al-jadalī* [The Koran in the Light of Dialectical Materialism], Beirut 1972, pp. 97–8 and passim.

35. See the analysis of the overriding topos of unity in modern Arab

thought by W. Sharāra, *Baʿḍ mushkilāt ad-daula*, pp. 62ff.

36. D. Mac Rae, "Populism as an Ideology", in G. Ionescu and E. Gellner, eds, *Populism, Its Meaning and National Characteristics*, London 1969, pp. 155ff.

37. *Māʿalim fiṭ-ṭarīq* [Signposts], Cairo and Beirut 1981, p. 202.

38. For instance, *Al-ʿUrwa al-wuthqā*, Cairo 1958, pp. 130–31.

39. Ibid., pp. 155ff.

40. See details in Al-Azmeh, *Al-Turāth*, pp. 51ff.

41. Ibrahim, "Anatomy of Egypt's Military Islamic Groups", p. 441.

42. See the discussion of the whole question of "authenticity" in my *Al-Turāth*, pp. 11ff.

43. I refer the reader to the thoughts on these matters by B. Ghalioun in *Al-Masʿala al-qawmīya wa mushkilat al-aqallīyāt* [The National Question and the Problem of Minorities], Beirut 1979.

44. B. Etienne, *Algerie, culture et revolution*, Paris 1977, p. 41. The connection between the state and religion in Algeria was subject to a different evolution from that of the Mashriq. See particularly F. Colonna, "Cultural Resistance and Religious Legitimacy in Algeria", *Economy and Society*, 3, 1974, pp. 244ff.

45. For the economic conditions and pressures that gave rise to the involution out of which this insurrection was produced, see the excellent study of F. Lawson, "Social Bases for the Hamah Revolt", *MERIP Reports*, 12/9, 1982.

46. See principally T. Nairn, *The Break-up of Britain*, London 1977, pp. 339ff, 347.

4

Islamist Revivalism and Western Ideologies

The long-standing Islamist campaign against "imported ideas", "foreign ideologies" and other instances of national, moral, social or intellectual adulteration and impurity needs no deliberate documentation. I will regard it as a demonstrably constant trope in Islamist discourse, which is forever in pursuit of what it regards as fully authentic – that is, autochthonous sources for political, social and cultural action, as well as for thinking about such action. This source, a generic Islam which Islamism and especially salafism[1] has been constructing for a century and a half, is regarded as something self-evident, which is accessible to the natural faculties of any right-thinking individual. This is what salafism terms *fiṭra*,[2] for it regards Islam, after the prophetic *ḥadīth* (the *ḥadīth* is a corpus of narratives purporting to relate the sayings and actions of the Prophet), as the primeval religion, *din al-fiṭra*, a sort of natural religion in conformity with an implicit and unstated natural law. The human mind was capable of reaching correct moral and legal judgements in conformity with natural reason even before Revelation, and religions themselves develop along the lines of an evolutionist schema in which the judiciousness of natural reason is made more consummate and manifest.[3] Unsoiled by history, not subject to any substantive effect of temporality, this quest for purity presents itself as a fastidious and rigorous adherence to a body of textual material which excludes reference, or at least normative reference, to anything else: the Koran and the salutary precedent of fully creditable epigones – the Prophet, some other prophets and Muhammad's Companions, in addition to a small number of later figures, such as ʿUmar b. ʿAbd al-ʿAzīz, often referred to as Khāmis al-rāshidīn, the fifth of the Rāshidūn caliphs.

This body of textual reference to a utopia whose re-enactment today is put forward as the ultimate aim of salafism is at once narrative and performative,[4] providing a body of commands and exemplary actions of such absolute distinction and with such proximity to infallibility, that their very occurrence in the past constitutes a command for their re-enactment today.

It is this claim to fidelity to uṣūl – that is, the corpus of foundational texts, those of the Koran and the *ḥadīth* – that I wish to address. It is one which is sustained not by salafists alone, but by much of their audience, both sympathetic or otherwise. It is the case that this claim and its advocacy are taken at face value. Incredulity, however, is more beneficial, not only because of the anachronism that is immediately evident, but also because discourse is a coy object, much given to secrets, and utterly lacking in innocence. Texts are protean creatures; they remain inert and speechless so long as they have not been encoded. In order for texts to be culturally, socially and politically operative, which is what salafism requires of them, they must be encoded by the moment in which they are used. In other words, what must be sought in our investigation of the relationship between salafism and its sources, is the configuration of conceptual sources in terms of which the textual sources of Tradition are reclaimed.

One matter must be cleared up before the conceptual resources are pursued. Modern Islamic revivalism in the Arab World has recently bifurcated into a radicalism inspired by Pakistani Mawdudi (d. 1979) and the later Quṭb (executed in 1966), along with their common sources in medieval Hanbalite moralism and Wahhabite literalism, on the one hand, and the mainstream of reformist Islamic revivalism, exemplified by the Society of Muslim Brothers, on the other. The Society of the Muslim Brothers was born in Egypt at a time when social disaggregation and the conservative protest of threatened social groups were lent expression universally by forms of political organization associated with generic fascism: youth societies, scouting organizations with lofty moral values and with emphasis on discipline and adulation for the leader, conspiratorial para-military groups and ideologies of social exclusivism. The radical wing of this organization detached itself in the 1960s from the parent organization, which had been "sullied" by politics, and opted for direct action, mostly terrorism, in the cause of the integral establishment of utopia: the practice of the Prophet and his

Companions. Quṭb was one of the most influential voices in the advocacy of direct action, the preparation for which involves a detachment from society and the formation of an anti-society by a spiritual and intellectual elite which works for radical subversion. Mawdudi theorized the legitimacy of Pakistan, the formation of which had no ideological bases except for echoes of British notions of "indirect rule", and sought this in religion. His ideas, marginal at the outset, were made central by the regime of General Zia-ul Haq.

I shall assume for the moment that, in terms of the rules governing the discourse of each, the difference between them resides in their attitude to the translatability of traditional texts.[5] The hallmark of Islamist modernism is its admission of the possibility, even the necessity of such translation: thus *shūra* becomes democracy, even parliamentary democracy; Islam becomes a charter for socialism; and the cosmic calamities indicated in the early, apocalyptic chapters of the Koran become premonitions of modern scientific discoveries. For the radicals, however, Islam is *sui generis*, and is utterly distinctive; it is therefore totally unrelated to democracy, especially parliamentary democracy, and any talk of relating it to socialism is polluting by implication, for the term "socialism" is contiguous with communism, and communism is atheistic, and neither socialism nor democracy occur in the Koran or salutary tradition. In radical Islamism, translation is precluded, and the utopia which is sought is a literalist one whose institutes have already been fully established. Fundamentalism here becomes, fully, *intégrisme*, not even precluding (for some radical groups) the reclamation of slavery. The present thus being no more than a shadow of unreality in comparison with the full ontological weight of the salutary example, it will be seen that such radical discourse rarely even adulterates itself with specifying matters arising in the present. Wahhabite discourse, for instance, rarely refers to its present, regarding it in some way as a register running parallel to itself, while it takes the form of a metonymic representation of present realities when it discourses on matters that occurred in the days of the Prophet.[6]

It has long been realized that Islamist revivalism is heavily impregnated with Western notions. This is perhaps most clearly so in the foundational texts of this revivalism to which reference is being made in this chapter: these are by ʿAbduh (d. 1905), Afghānī (d. 1897) and (to a lesser extent) Riḍā (d. 1935), who produced a repertoire of ideas which have infused Islamist discourse until the present. This is entirely unsurprising, given the circumstances of its emergence in the late nineteenth century in a milieu which was neither beholden to the religious hierarchy of the Azhar and similar institutions, nor particularly fond of it – Muhammad ʿAbduh spoke of decades spent in sweeping out of his head the filth deposited in it by Al-Azhar, then the major seat of Muslim learning in Egypt and beyond. ʿAbduh, Riḍā and their spiritual descendants spent considerable effort trying to translate Koranic and other traditional pronouncements into terms current in the political and scientific life of their days: ʿAbduh, in a very influential intepretation of a Koranic passage, pronounced the mysterious birds that devastated the army of the Ethiopian General Abraha on its approach to Mecca just before the birth of the Prophet to be, in all likelihood, a species of microbe-bearing mosquitoes.[7] Riḍā sometimes adopted the strategy of stating that historical and cosmic statements in the Koran out of keeping with modern knowledge were only meant approximately, and that their purpose was to edify above all else, not to instruct.[8] Both strategies are very common.[9]

In political and social matters, translation took the form of pairing various notions from tradition with matters of contemporary relevance. One of the major such notions is *shūrā*, consultation among Arab tribal grandees at the time of the Prophet, which was reclaimed as the fount and origin of popular presentation. As the political polemic of the early Islamic revivalists, such as ʿAbduh, 'Afghānī, Kawākibī and Riḍā has essentially been directed against despotism, this is hardly unsurprising; and in the course of its long career, the notion of *shūrā* has taken on many shades spanning the entire spectrum of the possibilities in Rousseau between direct democracy and a sort of sectoral senate containing representatives of various corporate and other groups. Other notions of the same order include the appropriation of socialism, especially under the Baathist and Nasserite regimes.

Along with notions of popular representation, the early Islamic revivalists took over other motifs of the Enlightenment. The question of how these motifs were acquired is still unsettled, and must remain so until the requisite research is done. What is demonstrable is that these ideas were very much in the air, and their genesis in an area of great cultural, political and ideological proximity – Young Ottoman thought.[10] Be that as it may, other

Enlightenment ideas that are evident in the revivalism of Afghānī, ʿAbduh and others are a notion very much akin to that of natural religion, in terms of which the primeval nature of Islam is articulated. Laroui has also indicated others: the refusal of any notions of historical immanence, a utilitarianism, a materialism in the methodological sense of pragmatism.[11] To these we must add the cardinal doctrine of the late nineteenth century, namely, evolutionism.

Evolutionism is deployed in many locations, not least that of the history of religion. Both Afghānī and ʿAbduh subscribed to the notion of an evolution of religion from animism through to idolatry to monotheism, which ran parallel to the intellectual evolution of humanity.[12] ʿAbduh adopted Spencer's notion of a societal evolution from a state of nature through to primary groupings and on to a political society. He also specifically rebutted the anti-Darwinist claim that the notion of natural selection was a subversive idea put forward by materialists, referring to a Koranic verse whose significance he elaborated in his exegesis.[13] However, the most important consequences of Darwinism and ideas associated with it for Islamic revivalism are more systematic and far more extensive than the impression one would gather from the treatment of Islamic revivalism of the details of the doctrine of evolution; for they go beyond the adoption of singular ideas at particular times in which they may be of wide incidence and acceptance, and constitute an articulated ideological orientation which has marked Islamic revivalism from its inception with Afghānī and ʿAbduh until the present. I refer to social Darwinism, which has marked the Islamist notions of society and of political action.

This social Darwinism must be explained in its origins and its persistence by more than direct conceptual influences – such as ʿAbduh's proclivity for Spencerian sociology (he had translated Spencer's *Education: Intellectual, Moral and Physical* [1861] from the French translation, but never published it), and the abiding impact of the work of the racist sociologist Gustave Le Bon in the Arab World, to name but a few instances.[14] More important is that this social Darwinism, with its attendant political Romanticism, is a common feature in the ideologies of all subaltern nationalisms or populisms. We would therefore be better advised to speak of convergence and the general circulation of ideas and of concordances and homologies. And, indeed, we find that the revivalism of

Afghānī and ʿAbduh was proto-nationalist, whereas what we might call neo-Afghanism, a nationalism of religious expression especially prevalent in Egypt in the past two decades, is a kind of hyper-nationalism which is unthinkable without the legacy of Arab nationalist ideology, especially Baathist nationalist discourse. In its train, revivalist ideology also implies a particular conception of history which connects late nineteenth-century revivalism with the neo-Afghanism of today.[15] I will now turn to these matters.

The collaborative effort between Afghānī and ʿAbduh which set the tone of all subsequent Islamic revivalism – the journal *al-ʿUrwa al-wuthqā* (published in Paris in the period March–October 1884) – sketches a coherent vitalist and social-Darwinist theory of society and of the relations between societies. This theory is very decidedly anti-Enlightenment both in its tenor and its content, and has been implicitly or explicitly embraced by all revivalist movements. The prime category in this notion of society is that of unity – and indeed, it has been very plausibly argued that the notion of unity is, in a Kantian sense, a "Form" of modern Arab historical understanding, or a category of modern Arab historical mind.[16] An organicist and vitalist model of the body politic is proffered. A society in health is one in which its various components – individual and corporate – are functionally interdependent and in accord regarding the purpose, or the teleological terminus, of that society, which is to be a polity; and no polity is consummate until it has proved capable of subjugating others.

In contrast, a body politic (*milla*) in which the various parts are not related by a purposeful unity resembles a body in distemper. Like a body in distemper, a body politic whose components are not co-ordinated and convergent is one from which the vital pneumatic impulse or the unifying soul is being diminished. Like a body on the point of death, once the soul or the preservative spirit of this unity is gone, the form of this body politic (*umma*) wanes, although its component parts may yet remain.[17]

There is much that is medieval about this model. Indeed, most of its notions are derived from medieval Islamic natural philosophy in which Afghānī – though not ʿAbduh – was very well versed. Terms such as Light, *hayūlā* (*hyle*), substance, active intellect, soul, entelechy and others abound both in the ʿ*Urwa* and in Afghānī's writings. So much alive were these matters in the mind of Afghānī that he even felt it necessary to take a position on a medieval polemic concerning alchemy.[18] The application of natural-philosophical notions to the body politic account for Afghānī's fascination with Ibn Khaldūn. But I do not believe that it would be adequate for us to trace these notions to their medieval analogues. For Afghānī was writing and speaking, not in Qom, but in Cairo, Istanbul and Paris, and whatever intellectual leaven he used, the reception of his ideas – and their abiding influence – must surely derive from other conditions. Ideas of political organism were prevalent, under the pervasive influence of Spencer, and shared by secular Arab thinkers of the time, such as Shumayyil.[19] The Rousseauian notion of the general will plausibly invites this gloss. A comparison that also naturally comes to mind is one with Herder's vitalist Romanticism which is also traceable in Young Ottoman thought.[20] The infusion of the body politic, the political organism, with a vital force which permeates and empowers its individual parts is an idea analogous to Herder's *Kräfte* as inner sources of vitality and dynamic principles for the continued existence of nations. Also in common with Herder, the Afghānī–ʿAbduh paradigm concretizes this vital principle for the unity and cohesion of bodies politic in culturalist terms which, like Herder's emphasis on *Bildung*, finds in moral Islamic education an anchor for the altruism which is vital for the continued political existence of the body politic. I am not implying that Afghānī or ʿAbduh may have borrowed from Herder, but that Herder's thought simply represents a paradigm for Romantic nationalism throughout the nineteenth and twentieth centuries. This paradigm is in many respects apparent in what has been termed the "solidaristic corporatism" of Zip Gökala (d. 1924),[21] the main theoretician of Turkish nationalism at the turn of the century. It also became a primary feature of Arab nationalist ideology in the interwar period, and then crystallized into Baathism, and also into the political theory of the Syrian Social Nationalist Party.

This vitalist model is supplemented by the Darwinist notion of the struggle for existence and the survival of the fittest, as was perfectly apposite for an observer of the way in which European powers were stalking and mauling the Ottoman Empire, and for observers of imperialism in the course of the present century. In one text, Afghānī tells his readers that "power is the manifestation of life and of existence ... and power is never manifest and concrete unless it weakens and subjugates others".[22] This model is portrayed quite cannibalistically in *Al-ʿUrwa al-wuthqā*,[23] where it is maintained that the power of a nation can only grow if it derived sustenance from a weaker one.

But where is Islam in all this? I must state here that the arguments of Afghānī and ʿAbduh require a constant effort of translation, for the arguments are constructed not by reference to some theoretical bases in political theory or in sociology, but to events in Islamic history, to the texts of the Koran, and elements in the *ḥadīth*. These in a way establish a foundation for the arguments without the necessity of explicit recourse to other forms of argumentation. In this sense, revivalism, the notion of *nahḍa*, is fully justified. The other sense of revivalism reveals to the observer a notion of history subjacent to the political and social philosophy whose elements have just been discussed, and this is a conception of history which is again prevalent among other populist and subaltern nationalist movements, but which has no textual or conceptual antecedents whatsoever in the Islamic tradition, and can only have been directly derived from Romanticism or its social and cultural conditions.

History in this context is seen as that of the unique historical subject and of other self-enclosed subjects. Each, and specifically Islam and the West, whatever these may mean, is self-enclosed, impenetrable in its essence, and is a substance presupposed by history rather than being its product. The passage of time is an alternation between true historicity manifested in might, and historical desuetude manifested in subjugation. Might results from cohesiveness and unity, and if this unity should be lost the body national will lose its spirit or its general will (a very Rousseauian phrase) with the result that "the thrones of its might will fall, and it [the nation] will take its leave of existence just as existence has abandoned it".[24]

The cohesiveness and unity of this body national infused with a vital impulse that yearns for glory is maintained so long as the factors which originally constituted this *Volksgeist* are operative. But once corruption sets in, once the essence is diluted, the auguries of national calamity become manifest. Thus Afghānī thought, for instance, that the glorious classical civilization of the Muslim Arabs was corroded from the inside by the snares of esotericist sects, which paved the way for conquest by Crusaders and Mongols. Similarly, the fabric of the Ottoman Empire was weakened by Ottoman Westernizing reformists in the middle of the nineteenth century. As for the French, the glory of their royal past was corrupted by the seductions of Voltaire and Rousseau, which directly led to what he regarded as the calamities of the French Revolution, the Paris Commune and defeat in the Franco–Prussian War.[25]

There is no positive response to such weaknesses and destruction save that of revivalism: the retrieval and restoration of the original qualities that made for strength and historical relevance. No progress without the retrieval of pristine beginnings and the cleansing of the essence from the adulterations of history: such is the fundamental principle of revivalism, and the trope in which intersect the enterprises of salafism as a return to the prescriptions of the texts and the political, proto-nationalist project of revivalism. That which is being revived is the essence of the body politic once powerful, as inscribed in the texts that are its putative foundations, in institutional and moral terms. As for historical change, it can, according to this model, be described only as privations of this original essence, as adulterations which in no way sully the purity of the foundation, adulterations which are anyway the work of foreigners, malcontents or other subversives: esotericist sects, Persians, Turks, Westernized elites. The alternance of history between might and powerlessness, glory and abjectness, is also one between authenticity and inauthenticity, essential inwardness and external reference, original texts and imported ideologies, and ultimately between origins and corruptions of these origins, corruptions that do not, however, sully the abiding subliminal purity of the essential historical subject.[26]

I am not proposing that *Al-ʿUrwa al-wuthqā* is a foundational text for European fascist and National Socialist ideologies, but simply indicating a correspondence between the two. This correspondence goes further than a shared Romantic concept of history and a vitalist notion of the body politic or of nationality, and extends into the notion of political action.[27] In the real world, the notion of a historical subject which knows no essential dysfunction but only abeyance, must assert itself against history. Hence it must bring in its train an acute sense of voluntarism, for the will of the reformer or of the enlightened despot sought by Afghānī, for instance, stands to the weak nation as the intervention of a physician in the affairs of a body in distemper, restoring its nature to its essential course and consummation. And since the body politic is arbitrarily posited as *sui generis*, it follows that the liberty of the reformer is self-referential, tautological, one which accords well with Hegel's description of the absolute freedom claimed by Jacobinism:

the world becomes its own will, to which it relates in an unmediated fashion, and acts upon it as pure negation.[28]

It is this transcendental narcissism of the invariant historical subject which connects the proto-nationalism of early Islamic revivalism with the Islamist politics of today, as well as with the neo-Afghanism of previously left-wing intellectuals in the Arab World, especially in Egypt and among some Lebanese Shīʿītes. With the latter, as I have suggested earlier, a form of hypernationalism emerged in conjunction with the exhaustion of nationalist and socialist discourses as used by the nation-state that at the same time drew heavily both on Arab nationalist revivalism in its Baathist variety and on the conceptual repertoire of Marxism. As with revivalism its earlier forms, the translation of Islam into a new medium generates something quite other than Islam as it has developed over the past fourteen centuries, although this is not reason enough for us to deny its Islamism. Islam is therefore in the strict sense of the word a denomination. But naming is not an innocent activity, for in the context of ideological contestation names are criteria for differentiation, for political, social and cultural exclusion, and are therefore prime parameters of political action.

Revivalism and reformism are thus a Janus-like creature, with irrationalist revivalism coming more into prominence with today's neo-Afghanists. For them the leitmotif has become historical subjectivity, and Islam comes to play the role of the regulative principle which assures the putative continuity of this putative subject, one that, in the Kantian expression of Ḥassan Ḥanafī – the contemporary philosopher and author of a phenomenological interpretation of neo-Afghanism – for instance, assures autonomy as against the heteronomy attendant upon westernization.[29] Yet Ḥanafī and others maintain a constant ambiguity, for on the one hand they advocate transformations of society, polity and culture that could have been advocated by any Latin American Marxist political economist, while on the other they assimilate this to the notion of an independent and invariant historical subject as elaborated in *Al-ʿUrwa al-wuthqā*. In doing so, they proffer rather trite criticisms of what they regard as an invariant Western tradition whose metaphysical underpinnings, derived from materialism, render it incapable of accounting for other societies and other cultures. "Our" culture, by contrast, with utter disregard for historical and contemporary reality, is based on altruistic solidarities, and derives its metaphysical underpinnings as well as its social-scientific principles in some very mysterious way from belief in God.[30]

Notes

1. Salafism – a rendering of the Arabic *salafiyya* – is a generic term which corresponds in meaning and intention to fundamentalism. It calls for a return to the Koran and the salutary example of pious epigones (the *salaf*). This representation of Islam owes its intellectual force to a long tradition of traditionalist piety which was latent yet almost invariably marginal. Its intellectual foundations were laid by a group of formidable Hanbalite intellectuals, particularly in thirteenth-century Damascus, and it was taken over, in a much impoverished form, as the leitmotif of the Wahhabite reform of the eighteenth and nineteenth centuries, which led to the foundation of Saudi Arabia.

2. See, for instance, Muhammad Rashīd Riḍā, *Muḥāwarat al-muṣliḥ wa'l-muqallid* [Dialogue between a Traditionalist and a Reformist], Cairo AH 1324, pp. 64 and passim, and the analysis of ʿAlī Umlīl, *Al-Islāḥīya al-ʿArabīya wa'd-dawla al-Waṭanīya* [Arab Reformism and the National State], Beirut and Casablanca 1985, pp. 58–61.

3. See, for instance, Rifāʿa Rāfiʿ al-Ṭaḥṭāwī, *Al-Aʿmāl al-Kāmila* [Complete Works], Beirut 1970, vol. 2, pp. 479, 481; Muhammad ʿAbduh, *Al-Aʿmāl al-Kāmila* [Complete Works], Beirut 1972, vol. 3, pp. 447–50. This matter, with Muʿtazilite antecedents, also invites comparison with the distinction made by European natural right theories between *ius gentium* and *ius civile*.

4. On utopianism in this context, see Aziz Al-Azmeh, "Utopia and the State in Islamic Political Thought", *History of Political Thought*, XI, 1990, pp. 9–20, and this volume, ch. 5.

5. Cf. Umlil, *Al-Iṣlāḥīya*, pp. 164ff.

6. Aziz Al-Azmeh, "Wahhabite Polity", in Ian Richard Netton, ed., *Arabia and the Gulf: From Traditional Society to Modern States*, London 1986, pp. 84–5, and this volume ch. 6.

7. ʿAbduh, *Aʿmāl*, vol. 5, p. 529.

8. Muhammad Rashīd Riḍā, *Fatawi Muhammad Rashid Rida* [Edicts of Muhammad Rashīd Riḍā], Beirut 1970–71, no. 54. This approach was consummately stated by Muḥammad Aḥmad Khalaf Allāh, *Al-Fann al-qiṣaṣī fi'l Qur'an* [Narrative Art in the Koran], 2nd edn, Cairo 1975, which provoked an anathema from Al-Azhar.

9. See, in general, Malcolm Kerr, *Islamic Reform*, Berkeley and Los Angeles 1967; and Abdallah Laroui, *L'Idéologie arabe contemporaire*, Paris 1967.

10. Şerif Mardin, *The Genesis of Young Ottoman Thought. A Study in the Modernization of Turkish Political Ideas*, Princeton 1962.

11. Abdallah Laroui, *Islam et modernité*, Paris 1987.

12. ʿAbduh, *Aʿmāl*, vol. 1, pp. 281–7, 337; vol. 4, pp. 558–61; Muhammad Rashīd Riḍā, *Tarikh al-Ustadh al-imam Muhammad ʿAbduh*, [Biography of Muhammad Abduh], vol. 1 (Cairo AH 1350/AD 1931–32) pp. 52–3; Salīm ʿAnḥūri, Siḥr Hārūt, Damascus 1302/1885, pp. 1177–8. These notions were shared with secular thinkers of the day, who imbibed the same conceptual material: for instance, Shiblī Shumayyil, *Taʿrīb li-Sharh Büchner ʿalā madhhab Darwin* [Translation of Büchner's Commentary on Darwin's Doctrine], Alexandria 1884, pp. h–t, m; and Shumayyil, *Majmūʿ-at al-Duktūr Shiblī al-Shumayyil*, [Collection of Dr Shibli Shumayyil], vol. 2, Cairo 1910, pp. 85–8.

13. *Al-Manār*, 8/24 10 February 1906, pp. 929–30.

14. See the comments on the influence of right-wing European ideas on Arabic thought by Raʾif Khuri, *Modern Arab Thought.*

15. See Aziz Al-Azmeh, "The Discourse of Cultural Authenticity: Islamist Revivalism and Enlightenment Universalism", in Eliott Deutsch, ed., *Culture and Modernity*, Honolulu 1991, and "Islamism and Arab Nationalism", *Review of Middle East Studies*, 4, 1988, pp. 45–7 (this volume chs 2 and 3).

16. Waḍḍaḥ Sharāra, *Ḥawla baʿḍ mushkilāt ad-dawla fiʾl-thaqāfa waʾl-mujtumaʿ al-ʿarabiyyain*, pp. 62–71, 16.

17. *Al-ʿUrwa al-wuthqā*, Cairo 1965, pp. 40–42, 33, 59–60, 78, 81 and passim; see Al-Azmeh, "The Discourse of Cultural Authenticity".

18. Jamāl ad-Dīn al-Afghānī, *Al-Aʿmāl al-kāmila*, [Complete Works], Cairo, n.d., pp. 213–8.

19. Shumayyil, *Majmūʿa*, pp. 2, 35ff.

20. Mardin, *Genesis*, pp. 355–6.

21. Taha Parla, *The Social and Political Thought of Ziya Gökalp, 1876–1924*, Leiden 1985, pp. 29–33, 42, 46.

22. Afghani, *Aʿmāl*, pp. 443–4.

23. Ibid., p. 74.

24. Ibid., p.153.

25. Ibid., pp. 157–64.

26. On the revivalist conception of history, see Al-Azmeh, "The Discourse of Cultural Authenticity", this volume, ch. 2.

27. Ibid.

28. Hegel, *Phenomenology of the Spirit*, transl. A.V. Miller, Oxford 1977, paras 584, 590, 593.

29. *Dirāsāt falsafiya* [Philosophical Studies], Cairo 1988, p. 52.

30. Most notably, the attempt to create "autochthonous" social science by ʿĀdil Ḥusain, *Nahw fikr ʿarabi jadīd.*

5

Utopia and Islamic Political Thought

It is easy to underestimate the complexity of utopia in Islamic political thought, the diversity and variety of elements it calls forth to the mind with and without justification. It is easy not fully to appreciate the problems attendant upon ascribing to Islamic political thought a utopian element, not least because the notion of utopia is itself problematic and easy to banalize, and because in Islam utopian elements are elusive and difficult to disentangle from mythological, eschatological, legal and didactic contexts. More important, in addressing the question of utopia and the state in Islamic political thought, one has to confront the problematic status of political thought in Islam, and one must try to approach it in a way other than by analogy with modern political thought. Islamic political thought is a topic much addressed, but very little understood, and the general impression one gains from modern studies is one of essentialism, recursivity and repetitiveness[1] – there are exceptions of course. So one must reflect, in however preliminary a form, upon the notion of Islamic political thought, which is really not so much a coherent, deliberate and disciplined body of investigation and inquiry concerning a well-defined and delimited topic, but is rather an assembly of statements on topics political, statements dispersed in various discursive locations; there is no "political theory" as such in Islamic political thought.

This contribution will therefore scan a period of over a thousand years and probe the edges and boundaries of its subject matter; it hopes to offer a number of specifications, distinctions and notions which are essential if one were to be able to begin thinking about utopia in Islamic political thought. Impressing upon the reader the importance and necessity of these preliminary distinctions and specifications will, in itself, be a worthwhile task. Of these specifications I will start with one which I have already elaborated elsewhere.[2] This concerns the state – *dawla* in Arabic. Both lexically and in terms of actual usage until modern times, the term denoted a particular kind of patrimony, the proprietorship of command and authority within a specific line. Very rarely is the state, *dawla*, actually discussed – as distinct from being mentioned – in works that concern politics, be they works of public law, of ethics, or *Fürstenspiegel*. The precise field of use and elaboration of the term and the notion *dawla* is historical literature.[3] In historical writing, *dawla* refers to the continuity over time of power exercised by a string of successive sovereigns, and to the facility by which single sovereigns exercise exclusive power: thus we have the *dawla* of the Abbasids, and the *dawla* of Hārūn al-Rashīd. This abstract *dawla* is constituted of a body politic, in the original sense: a sovereign, his troops, his bureaucrats. What must be stressed is that this concrete body is distinct from a body social and from what later came to be known as civil society. This is absent from Islamic political thought except as an abstract locus of order and disorder which receives the action of *dawla*, and is only implicitly conceived in Islamic law. *Dawla* only relates to that which stands apart from it in a very abstract fashion; in this connection the sovereign, *sultān*, is the sole political subject, whose action upon society is univocal.[4] The exclusivity and totality of sovereign power is habitually compared to that of God, not unlike the practice in pre-modern European traditions. In Mamluk times, for instance, the jurist Ibn Jamāʿa (d. 1333) carried through an interesting transposition which elevated the force of this analogy: whereas dogmatic theologians had previously demonstrated the unicity and omnipotence of God by, among other things, analogy with the unicity and omnipotence of royal power, he demonstrated these same characteristics of royal power by analogy with the divinity.[5]

The state in this context is therefore little more than the everyday incarnation of power, the monopoly of abstract power to command and coerce. We must, incidentally, view the notions of the celebrated Ibn Khaldūn (d. 1406) in this context: whereas it is still the common wisdom on this matter that Ibn Khaldūn was in essence a sociologist who derived state from society, close textual scrutiny and attention to that which is thinkable and unthinkable in his historical world would reveal that it is abstract power, not society, which is the primary substance of his discourse.[6]

One derivative of power is the field of its use: politics, *siyāsa* in Arabic. *Siyāsa* denotes absolutist management, the direction by reason of unreason. It is used in relation to animal husbandry. It is the management of natural disorder by the order of culture, and regal power is the ultimate state of culture in a natural world of men marked by a *bellum omnium contra omnes* which necessitates the establishment of power – this power is variously termed *wāziʿ* (Ibn Khaldūn), *wazʿa* (Jāhiz – d. 869), *shawka* (Ghazālī – d. 1111, Juwainī – d. 1085), *qahr* (Ibn Jamāʿa) and *ghalaba* and *taghallub* (Ibn Taimiyya – d. 1327), or generally *mulk* and *sultān*. *Siyāsa* is therefore not the field where power is contested and arrived at: *siyāsa* presupposes the power of which it is a *modus operandi*. It is true that Muslim writers on politics from the earliest times like Ibn al-Muqaffaʿ in the eighth century, to Ibn Khaldūn more than six hundred years later, adopted some Persian notions and distinguished between three types of kingship and of *siyāsa*: that based on religion, that based on reason, and that based on caprice.[7] This is not a typology of state forms as is sometimes maintained, but is an operationalist classification of *siyāsa*. *Siyāsa*, politics, does not establish power and authority, but presupposes it and is premised on its absolutist exercise. The relation of all these notions to political and historical reality is an interesting matter, but I must resist the temptation to discuss it now.

Be that as it may, in Arab-Islamic writings pertaining to politics, *siyāsa* is of course encountered in two types of discourse. The first is the flourishing *Fürstenspiegel* genre, the tradition of which persisted from Sassanian times well into the Ottoman Empire. The principles of *siyāsa* in this body of writing consisted of sententious statements and of *exempla* which could best be reclaimed from the past for advertence, exhortation and emulation. The repetition of these *exempla* amounts to the repetition of movements by which skills are acquired, and these books are in effect technical manuals, not theoretical treatises on the science of politics.[8] This was indeed appropriate to the circumstances, for these texts were normally delivered at court orally, and oral education proceeds by means of narratives and proverbs rather than by more general statements – this is as true of the Abbasid court as of Cathar education studied by Le Roy Ladurie or education based upon the Homeric epic studied by Havelock.[9] Central among the topics addressed in these *Fürstenspiegel* is *ʿadāla*, justice – this was not here a legal category of course, but a descriptive notion denoting a harmonious arrangement of things in such a way that everything would remain in its place. Their result would thus be optimally beneficial to the king. At the centre of this just and harmonious order is hierarchy: a just manner of management is just when it guides the affairs of men in a way commensurate with how things turn out to be in terms of their relations of hierarchy – the argument is circular, but it is not mine, and circularity is here concomitant with the attitude of hyper-realism such as that professed by *Fürstenspiegel.*

The other type of discourse on *siyāsa* is the one where we will have our first encounter with the notion of utopia: this is *siyāsa sharʿiyya*, that based on *Sharʿ*, the Islamic *nomos*, the *dharma* of the Muslims. This, like that of the *Fürstenspiegel*, is anchored in the prior assumption of absolute power, and is another *modus operandi* of power. The discourse is primarily legal discourse. It is perhaps necessary at the outset to correct an assumption often made in modern scholarship, which supposes that *siyāsa sharʿiyya* is a late development, consequent on the atrophy of the caliphate and to be set in Saljuq and Mamluk times.[10] Henri Laoust has quite correctly taken it further into the past than is normally thought, and described the *Ahkām sultāniyya* of the eleventh century Māwardī (d. 1058) as a work of *siyāsa sharʿiyya.*[11] I would take it three centuries further back to the time when the *sharīʿa* was still in genesis as a distinct body of ideological and legal motifs, and specifically to the suggestion by Ibn al-Muqaffaʿ (d. 759) that the Abbasid Caliphate should suppress legal differences and institute a body of statutes by which they would regulate the affairs of the world. In other words, there is not a phase of unadulterated religious polity in Islamic history, nor was there ever this presumption by Muslim politicians or jurists.

Moreover, the *sharʿī* character of *siyāsa* is not altogether formally distinct from the notion of justice just discussed, though it is distinct in provenance and in its substantive details. Formally, like the *exempla* of the *Fürstenspiegel*, these details are premised as pregiven power and authority, and are so constituted as a particular means of administration and the husbandry of human beings in their private and collective lives. They are, as the titles of countless treatises tell us, *aḥkām*: statutes, ordinances, judgements, rulings.

In provenance, they emanate in part from divine and otherwise revered commands and interdictions as manifested in the Koran and in narratives about sayings and actions of Muhammad, and in part from the varied and sometimes discordant rulings or jurists and early Muslims. These, together with the small amount of explicit legislation attributed to divine and prophetic origin, constitute the body of Islamic law. It has been suggested that the *sharīʿa* in this context is a remote ideal, unrealizable and therefore, in the banal sense, utopian. Recently the proposition has been put forward that it was the ideal of the caliphate, as overseer of the *sharīʿa* and vicar of prophecy, that constitutes the utopianism of Islamic political theory.[12] It was proposed in addition that so unrealizable was this that it left ample space for the social and political opportunism of the elaborators of this utopianism, the politically quietist *ʿulamāʾ*: the ideal caliphate can not be denied in principle, nor affirmed in reality.

The essential distinction that is being made here is between the caliphal ideal and political reality, be this reality associated with the caliphate as under the Abbasids, or with a non-caliphal form of royal sovereignty, as that under, say, the Mamluks. The distinction is not novel, though the imputation of utopianism is. It corresponds to the traditional theses of Orientalist studies, and these are based less on a proper consideration of historical realities than on the selective incorporation of these realities within the *topoi* and rhetorical conventions which constitute the fundamental working material of these studies in the form which still predominates today – though I must stress that this predominance has not been without serious challenge in the past decade or two. Axial among the presuppositions of this tradition of scholarship is that the *sharīʿa* is an unambiguous body of rulings, at one and the same time all-embracing and definitively normative and, above all, a moment of divinity. It is, for Tilman Nagel, "die in Buchstaben geronnene Form" of the divinely willed order.[13] For him, collective life in Islam is the divinely ordained form of human society.[14] Louis Gardet calls this fantasy "the Islamic city", which he describes as an ideal type which has no existence.[15] The same is repeated by other works. Thomas Arnold[16] imagined that theories of government had their consummate beginnings very early on, in the Medinan period at the very beginning of Islam, naturally enough with no reference to reality.

It is this presumed divorce from reality, this gratuitous, dreamy quality, which is underlined. The *sharīʿa* in its political and social moment is, according to the theses under discussion, the sole legitimate regulator of mundane life for extra-mundane ends. By the same token, it is utopian. There is little merit in this supposition. In the first place, the *sharīʿa* is the nominal umbrella of a variety of different things and is by no means univocal. The majority of its rulings do not have the finality attributed to them by modern studies. With few exceptions, Islamic law is a body of differences and of general rulings. The great works of public law and governmental statutes, such as those of Māwardī and Abū Yaʿlā (d. 1066),[17] are themselves with few exceptions highly multivocal. On the various points they elaborate they adduce a multiplicity of conflicting precedents, rulings, deductions, all of which are considered equally legitimate, and the caliph is called upon to pronounce legal preference, in much the same way as jurists do – and a precondition for the caliphate is juristic competence. Ultimately, the supposition I am contesting here is inscribed in the *topos* of decline according to which Islamic history is imagined in standard textbooks and which holds, among other things, that the untenable ideals of the beginning give way to reality until the former, according to Gibb and Rosenthal,[18] give way completely to the latter, with which it is by definition, almost by a force of nature, in contradiction and dissonance. The essentially flawed utopian ideal is refuted, but in their inveterate folly Muslims somehow keep on cherishing it, as a dreamy utopia, making it the object of curiosity rather than of historical, political or ideological analysis.

This same idea is also pitched at another level. Laroui maintains that the application of the *sharīʿa*, that is, the institution of *siyāsa sharʿiyya*, denotes the legality of the state, but is not sufficient for this state to be legitimate.[19] This distinction is an adaptation of a Khaldūnian distinction between kingship and the true caliphate. According to this precept, the true caliphate was a miraculous irruption which was perverted and degenerated into mere kingship. This distinction, incidentally, derived less from the tradition of Sunni political or historical thought than from the cyclism of chiliastic sufism current in the Maghreb and the Andalus in the Middle Ages.[20] It is premised by Laroui on the unobjectionable proposition that a legal state is nothing but a natural state, a mundane, profane creature, which adopts the *sharīʿa* as its legal system.[21] Also adapting Ibn Khaldūn, who in this case rehearses a thesis which was then well established, though it was not as constant a refrain as one would expect from modern commentaries, Laroui maintains that the only political order which is legitimate as well as legal is the pristine caliphate – the regime at Medina, whose appearance was miraculous and which, by the nature of things, was of short duration.[22] It was also in the nature of a regime such as this, and of society whose instrument it is, to teach the individual member, whose duty it is to transcend himself and his natural condition, in order to become akin to the ideal man whose perfect example is the Prophet Muhammad: the aim of this state is therefore beyond society, and "l'Islam ne quitte pas ... le royaume des fins". It is herein that utopia lies.[23]

This point will, however, be pursued without reference to either the term or the notion of legitimacy, for it is one which is ill-fitting in relation to Islamic political thought: legitimacy is a notion relating, in distinct ways, to dynastic and other forms of agnatic integrity, and to representative government. It is hence at best peripheral in Sunni Islamic political thought, which as we saw is concerned with the administration and violent regulation of an order whose hinge is a pre-established power, although the identity of imperfection and illegitimacy can be imputed to some strands of Shiʿite dogma. The following account will therefore join the almost universal consensus of Muslim scholars and regard all political regimes to be legitimate as long as they do not actually foster systematic hostility to Islamic law.

Ibn Taimiyya, who is always direct and explicit in the statement of his assumptions as well as those of others, excavates and brings forth a position often stated by others but left unvalorized and in an emblematic isolation: that a *milla*, a community of believers, is not simply one form of polity among others. Ibn Taimiyya emphasizes this in order to reject a correlated proposition, that prophecy is merely a form of just *siyāsa* granted to mankind for the proper conduct of mundane life.[24] This holds without regard to the nature of a regime based on the *sharʿ* and whether it be caliphal or sultanic. Whereas Māwardī[25] and Ibn al-Jawzī (d. 1201),[26] for instance, reflecting general consensus, asserted that the *sharʿī* order guaranteed and managed by the caliphate is instituted for the good order of the world and of religion. Ibn Taimiyya assimilates the former to the latter: he establishes an exclusive primacy of divine purpose which leads to the identity of the mundane order with it – if this order be based on *sharʿ*.

The key to this reduction is a specific form of traditionalism, *salafiyya* – the contemporary term is fundamentalism, or *intégrisme* in France: the one term derived from the traditions of Protestantism, the other of Catholicism. In *salafī* traditionalism the ultimate in exemplary tradition and utopian model is that which can be attributed to the prophetic example and that of his associates and some of their early successors, in addition to some central figures of universal recognition and exemplitude, such as Aḥmad b. Ḥanbal (d. 855). Though neither holy nor divine, this body of exemplars, conveniently called the Medinan regime, is in some way – by miracle or by direct communion – evidence of the transitivity of the divinity. It is in full conformity with divine purpose and ordinance – it is indeed the manifestation of this purpose and ordinance. It is an instance of unalloyed perfection; the literary critic Northrop Frye, writing two decades before *glasnost*, described utopian discourse as one in which the utopian location is inspected under the guidance of a sort of Intourist guide.[27] Indeed, writings on prophetic biography as on the Medinan regime have this quality to a very appreciable degree, and it is this history which constitutes the material of *salafī* utopia. This is utopia in the strict sense of something which exists elsewhere, rather than an atopia which exists nowhere – and I say "elsewhere" mindful of the anachronism which this may bring to mind – yet temporality is not an element of the primitivist traditionalism which is *salafiyya*, for this is really premised on the denial of temporality, or at least of its cumulativeness, and is equally premised on the reversibility of time.

Of course, *salafı* traditionalism is not confined to what it is convenient to call fundamentalism (I define fundamentalism as that moment in all religions which gives primitivism and primevalism precedence over history, which seeks to eliminate history and regard it as, at best, an illegitimate accretion onto the pristine beginning, and as such regard the present condition and its immediate precedents as corrupt, or at best as corruptions of an abiding beginning): this notion is, of course, shared with all other movements with claims to revivification, notably nationalism and populism. The primitivist vitalism of these tendencies is reflected in the names they have taken, and of these I need mention only the Risorgimento and the Baath. I think this is a crucial point to bear in mind when thinking of contemporary Muslim radicalism. In terms of this traditionalism, history is the history of corruption and of decay. Primitivism and utopia here are one; the ideal is historically concrete and always immanent, and the task is for its restoration or re-enactment.

But for historical as distinct from fundamentalist Islam, for the Islam that was and is lived as distinct from that of fantasy both medieval and modern, for the Islam that took account of the work of time, the Islam of *ijmāʿ* (consensus) and *ikhtilāf* (difference with mutual recognition), whose legal theory regards its own judgements as only probable regardless of their practical necessity and compulsion[28] – in other words, for the Islam that represents the experience of the overwhelming majority of Muslim peoples, terrains and histories, the consequences of the corruptive influence of time are not drawn with any consistency. Primitivism here is ideologically piecemeal and whimsical, with a moralistic rather than a political valorization. Exemplary history, the history of the Medinan regime, is a quarry of precedents elaborated within the body of legislation and of legal discourse concerning public affairs.[29] The Medinan regime is the true Golden Age which should be approximated in so far as this is possible in an imperfect world, and a situation which is only repeatable under determinate circumstances to which I will address myself in due course. This is not a totalitarian utopia, therefore, in any consummate sense, but a utopia in terms of the here and now: an elsewhere, some examples from which can be made into legal statutes for the here and now; a moral, didactic utopia, with practical use in jurisprudence, but not repeatable in its totality, and therefore not involving political engagement. In other words, in historical Islam the primitivist moment is a myth, in the classic sense of the charter of a ritual in which the status quo is dramatized, not overturned; accomplished, not sought.

Utopia in the fuller sense emerges in the fundamentalist moment: the Medinan regime may well be a unique phenomenon, but its purity and integrality can be re-established, and its institutes constitute a programme of political and social action whose actuality, though not palpable, is yet possible. Indeed, Ernst Bloch quite rightly stated that utopian ideas, which might be likened to a child's dream about presents, induce a rhapsodic enthusiasm which carries the dreamer beyond considerations of means. This same condition can keep its holder restless and expectant, full of life and striving. Otherwise put, again following Bloch but with some adaptation this time, utopia in this instance is not only a device for voyeuristic palliation, but a vital stimulus.[30]

The Medinan Caliphate can thus be regarded, with Laroui, as a utopia. What Laroui omits is an important complement without which consideration of this matter would remain incomplete: this is eschatology. Unlike activist, fundamentalist utopia, this finalist state of felicity and rectitude associated with the future reigns of the Mahdī (the Messiah) and of ʿĪsā b. Maryam (Jesus Christ) is not the result of voluntaristic action. Like the Medinan regime and the prophetic example, it is a miraculous irruption by divine command onto the face of history, although it will be announced for the believers by many cosmic and other signs. Not only is the End a recovery of the Muslim prophetic experience, it is also the recovery of the primordial Adamic order, of the line of Abel, of every divine mission like those of Noah, Abraham, Moses, David, Solomon, Jesus and Muhammad, who incorporates, transcends and consummates them all in the most definitive form of primeval religiosity, Islam. The End, like the beginning and like the periodic irruptions of prophecy, is really against nature; it is the calque of the beginning so often repeated in history, and is the ultimate primitivism.[31]

Eschatology and past example become utopia when they become activist, when they become a chiliasm, with a sense of total imminence. They become utopia when legalism and moralism give way to total political contestation. This occurs when the fundamentalist moment as distinct from historical Islam is ascendant among particular groups in society. Islamic political and social ideals based on primitivist models become utopian when these models are activated and valorized, when fundamentalism ceases to be a cliché and takes on programmatic specifications and, as a precondition of this specification, acquires a social and political constituency. Historically, this has taken two main forms. In the Islamic Middle Ages, radical fundamentalism was, as far as I know, invariably chiliastic, associated with the complex of ideas generically known as Mahdism. North African history is especially replete with Mahdism both Sunnite and Shiʿite: the Idrīsids, the Fāṭimids, the Almohads, Sufi politics like that of Ibn Qasī (d. 1151), a thaumaturge who established a short-lived state in the Algarve, and countless others. These have already been mentioned briefly, and associated with Ibn Khaldūn's theory of kingship.

The second form of activist utopianism is contemporary Islamic radicalism, for which there is no precedent in Islamic history. Like chiliasm, it relies on the specification of fundamentalism, that is to say, on the precise and imminent interpretation of the pristine model, be that divine pronouncement or utopian example. This is quite natural in all utopias, for by their very nature these have to establish a constituency by affirming the univocality of texts and examples which are, in themselves, naturally multivocal:[32] Plato specified his Republic in the *Laws*, Rousseau his Contract with his projected Corsican constitution.

Similarly, Islamic radicalism, a very recent phenomenon indeed and the illegitimate offspring of Islamic reformism and Wahhabite-Mawdudian fundamentalism, was born of a particular specification. It specified *jāhilīyya*, the non-Islam that is to be converted into Islamic order, as an actual presence. Of course each movement in this fundamentalism produced particular specifications consonant with its social, political and cultural import. Wahhabite fundamentalism in Arabia, from the beginning until the definitive establishment of utopia by the Imam (later King) ʿAbd al-Azīz (the foundation of Saudi Arabia) and the suppression of the Ikhwān Wahhabite militia in 1927, decreed all territory identified for absorption by the expanding Saudi polity as *jāhilīyya* – and by territory I mean geographical territory to be subjugated, socio-political territory to be linked to the House of Saud in a tributary fashion, and of course religious territory defined by the diversity of local cults whose centralization and homogenization under the title of *Sharīʿa* was a cultural precondition for political centralization.[33] *Sharīʿa* here is of course in the main Hanbalite, characterized by a moralistic rigour which homogenizes public life on the one hand, and an economic liberalism on the other, much like some early Protestant polities.

Yet the suppression of the Ikhwān in Saudi Arabia was not the end of the story. Once the *jāhilīyya* was overcome, the utopian motif did manage to sustain itself in roughly the same way as it had over many centuries – as somewhat fulfilled in the institutes of government, in the uncontested circus games occasionally on offer in main squares of Saudi cities after Friday prayers, in the motifs of the state cultural and educational system. Each of these was a glimpse into the utopian beyond daily forced into the imagination, most especially of theology students. Yet in contrast to previous times of activism, the utopian model in Saudi Arabia, and especially the anti-utopia, was hardly specified: it referred to remote matters like communism and the Soviet threat, more of pertinence to the US perspective in the cold war than to Arabian matters. It is a remarkable though typical fact that fundamentalist texts – the works of Muhammad b. ʿAbd al-Wahhāb and of his commentators, for instance – are highly unspecific: they speak of *jāhilīyya*, of *shirk*, of unbelief, of various iniquities, not in terms of contemporary indication but of events, personalities, conditions and sayings which purportedly took place in early Islamic times. Reality as perceived today is an implicit gloss, a parallel register of examples and anti-examples, each singly reducible to precedents of both rectitude and iniquity, each an expression, in code, of the other. They are, in a technical sense, tokens of each other.[34] Once the one is formally assimilated to the other, a practical activist programme emerges.

In this context there exists no difference between the general fundamentalist outlook of the chief official cleric in Saudi Arabia, the Sheikh ʿAbd al-ʿAzīz b. Bāz, and Juhaymān b. Muhammad al-ʿUtaibī, the leader of the chiliastic group which took over the enclosure of the Kaʿba in 1979. In his writings, Juhaimān b. Muhammad often refers, with great respect, to Ibn Bāz, and records that the cleric had seen and approved his writings. The only difference arose over specification: the utopia and its anti-type was for Ibn Bāz a textual outline at once abstract and hyper-concrete. He refused to join Juhaimān and his comrades in specifying the anti-type as the House of Saud, and in specifying the eschatological signs with which Saudi Arabia abounded as the actual occurrences that are referred to in Juhaimān's writings.[35] He was a signatory to the *fatwā obtained to execute the survivors after the holy enclosure was stormed.*

It was perhaps not unnatural that utopia in Saudi Arabia took on a messianic form; it reflects the relatively low level of cultural and political development of the country – though we must speak of backwardness with humility, in the light of the abiding irrationalism of political life in the West, evident in the currency of Nostradamus's prophecies of the apocalyptic political fantasy animating the American right and much foreign policy under the Reagan presidency, not to speak of the influence of Mrs Quigley on the White House. Elsehwere radical Islamism – as in Egypt, for instance, under the influence of thinkers like Sayyid Quṭb (d. 1965) and Abul-Aʿlā al-Mawdūdī (d. 1979) – displays utopia and the anti-utopia with a similar traditionalist literary mode. But the range of external references is of course much wider and denser, is far more concrete, and has absorbed much of the social and economic programmes of left-wing movements. When, for instance, Khālid al-Islambūlī and his associates assassinated Sadat, indications are that they were expecting to precipitate an uprising in order to locate utopia in Egypt, not the announcement of the advent of the Messiah. This represents the response of specific social, economic and cultural groups in Egypt to particular public circumstances which have been much discussed, and under the leadership of what I like to call the lumpenitelligentsia.[36]

The difference between Arabian and, say, Egyptian Muslim utopianism arises from distinct historical worlds to which they belong. Arabian utopianism imagines the chiliastic order in terms of miracle and without necessary political reference to the state; this is very much in keeping with medieval Islamic habits. Egyptian utopianism, on the other hand, regards its relation to the state as fundamental. It seeks immediately to take the state by force, as with the radicals professing notions like *takfīr.* It also seeks, as with the Muslim Brothers in their fundamentalist mode, to work a rhetorical reconciliation of the notion of *shūra* (a form of Medinan consultation) and of liberal political notions with the aim of gaining power. A similarly primitivist Islamism has gripped some sectors of the Middle Eastern intelligentsia, some of them of a Marxist background – the best known are perhaps Jalāl Al-ī Ahmad of Iran, and Muhammad ʿUmāra in Egypt. But what we have here is a very modern phenomenon – just as European evolutionism in the Enlightenment and the nineteenth century wedded utopia and natural law to produce evolutionism, these intellectuals have wedded theories of dependency with a Muslim primitivist utopia to produce what they call "the Muslim left". But I am of the firm opinion that what we have here is not an Islamic primitivism but shades of a hypernationalism, a different story altogether.

Notes

1. For instance, E.I.J. Rosenthal, *Political Thought in Medieval Islam*, Cambridge 1958; A.K.S. Lambton, *State and Government in Medieval Islam. An Introduction to the Study of Islamic Political Theory: The Jurists*, Oxford 1981.

2. A. Al-Azmeh, *Ibn Khaldūn: An Essay in Reinterpretation*, London 1982, pp. 26ff.

3. A. Al-Azmeh, *Al-Kītaba al-tārīkhīya wa'l ma'rifa al-tārīkhīya* [Historial Writing and Historical Knowledge], Beirut 1983, pp. 71ff.

4. W. Sharāra, "Al-Mulk/al-'āmma, al-tabī'a, al-mawt" [Kingship/Commoners, Nature and Death], *Dirāsāt 'Arabiyya*, XVI/12, 1980, pp. 19–47; Al-Azmeh, *Al-Turāth*, pp. 41ff.

5. Ibn Jamā'a, "Taḥrīr al-Ahkām", ed. H. Kofler, *Islamica*, VI, 1934, p. 365.

6. Al-Azmeh, *Ibn Khaldūn*, pp. 51–2, 155.

7. Ibn al-Muqaffa', *Al-Adab al-Kabīr wa'l adab al-Ṣaghīr* [The Greater and Lesser Disciplines], Beirut, n.d., p. 11.

8. Al-Azmeh, "Al-Siyāsa", p. 284; in general, see Rosenthal, *Political Thought*, ch. 3.

9. E.A. Havelock, *Preface to Plato*, Oxford 1963; E. Le Roy Ladurie, *Montaillou*, transl. B. Bray, Harmondsworth 1978, ch. XV.

10. Rosenthal, *Political Thought*, pp. 28 and passim; T.W. Arnold, *The Caliphate*, London 1924, pp. 67 and passim; H.A.R. Gibb, *Studies in the Civilization of Islam*, ed. S.J. Shaw and W.R. Polk, London 1962, pp. 143 and passim.

11. H. Laoust, "La Pensée et l'action politiques d'Al-Māwaradī (364/450–974/1058)', *Pluralismes dans l'Islam*, Paris 1983, pp. 190, 192 and passim.

12. A. Laroui, *Islam et modernité*, Paris 1987, ch. 1.

13. T. Nagel, *Staat und Glaubensgemeinschaft im Islam*, Zürich and Munich 1981, vol. 1, p. 13.

14. Ibid.

15. L. Gardet, *La Cité musulmane*, 2nd edn, Paris 1961, preface.

16. Arnold, *The Caliphate*, p. 25.

17. Māwardī, *Les Statuts governementaux*, transl. E. Fagnan, Algiers 1915, repr. Paris 1982; Abū Ya'lā, *Al-Ahkām al-Sultānīya* [Statutes of Government], ed. M.F. Fiqī, Cairo 1966.

18. Rosenthal, *Political Theory*, pp. 28, 33; Gibb, *Studies*, pp. 142, 151ff., 162.

19. Laroui, *Islam*, p. 26.

20. Ibn Khaldūn, *Les Prolégomènes*, ed. E. Quatremère, Paris 1858, vol. 1, pp. 375–6 and passim.

21. Laroui, *Islam*, pp. 21ff; Ibn Khaldūn, *Prolégomènes*, vol. 1, p. 344.

22. Laroui, *Islam*, pp. 26–7; Ibn Khaldūn, *Prolégomènes*, vol. 2, p. 249.

23. Laroui, *Islam*, p. 19.

24. Ibn Taimiyya, *Minhāj al-sunna al-nabawiyya fī naqd kalām al-Shī'a wa'l-Qadariyya* [Critique of Shia'a and Qaḍarite Doctrines According to Prophetic Pronouncements and Actions], Cairo AH 1322, vol. 1, p. 3.

25. Māwardī, *Al-Ahkām al-sultāniyya* [Statues of Government], Cairo 1973, pp. 3, 5.

26. Ibn al-Jawzī, *Al-Miṣbāh al-muḍī' fī khilāfat al-Mustaḍī'*, [The Brilliant Lamp on the Caliphate of Al-Mustaḍī'] ed. N.A. Ibrāhīm, Baghdad 1976–77, vol. 1, pp. 93–4.

27. N. Frye, "Varieties of Literary Utopia", in *Utopias and Utopian Thought*, ed. F.E. Mannell, Cambridge, MA 1966, p. 20.

28. H. Hanafi, *Les Méthodes d'exégèse*, Cairo 1965, pp. 165ff., 272ff; A. Al-Azmeh, *Arabic Thought and Islamic Societies*, London 1986, pp. 71ff.

29. An inventory of some of these is conveniently assembled in M.I. Faruqi, "Early Islamic History as a Model for the Development of Some Islamic Legal Categories', unpublished PhD thesis, University of Exeter, 1988.

30. E. Bloch, *A Philosophy of the Future*, transl. J. Cumming, New York 1970, p. 87.

31. Al-Azmeh, *Al-Kitāba al-Tārīkhīya*, pp. 107ff.

32. Cf. M. Le Doeuff, "Dualité et polysémie du texte utopique", *Le Discours utopique. Colloque de Cérisy*, Paris 1978, p. 333.

33. W. Sharāra, *Al-Ahl wa'l Ghanīma*; Al-Azmeh, "Wahhabite Polity", this volume, ch. 7.

34. Al-Azmeh, "Wahhabite Polity", this volume p. 115.

35. Below pp. 116–7

36. There are many works on radical Islamism, most of which are unreliable. For a judicious overview, see B. Johansen, *Islam und Staat, Abhängige Entwicklung, Verwaltung des Elends und religiöser Antiimperialismus*, Berlin 1982.

6

Wahhabite Polity

An Iraqi opponent of the Wahhabite movement[1] in the early part of the present century could not comprehend why the Wahhabites were bent on inverting the correct order of things, as he understood it, in terms of which the Ḥijāz and Najd were connected. Whereas the Najdī Wahhabites had considered the Ḥijāz to be territory to be conquered, subjugated and corrected, being technically *dār al-ḥarb*, it was in fact Najd (or rather the southern parts of it) which, in the early years of Islam, was the abode of the anti-prophet Musaylima, and was thus accursed territory that could in no way figure as *dār al-hijra*, as the Wahhabites claimed.[2] The repudiation of the irenical character of the mutually recognized and validated schools of Sunnī law was one of the charges most often levelled against the Wahhabites. Stress was laid on their radical intolerance of all but their own adepts to the extent of ascribing unbelief (*takfīr*) to all others, a feature that was often compared to the original position of the universally proscribed Kharijites,[3] and such stress was the substance of the very earliest critical pronouncements against the Wahhabites.[4] Muḥammad b. ʿAbd al-Wahhāb himself devoted a lengthy epistle to refuting, among other charges, the charge that he was seeking to transcend the four schools of Sunnī law,[5] and this charge seems to have been quite persistent, having been repeated in a threatening letter sent by the then Pasha of Damascus to Suʿūd b. ʿAbd al-ʿAzīz in 1808, in which the Ottoman official stated that the Wahhabites were ignorant bedouins without instruction in the fundamentals of the four schools.[6] There was indeed much confusion pertaining to the articles of Wahhabite belief, not to speak of events inside Najd; Muḥammad b. ʿAbd al-Wahhāb was accused of sorcery,[7] and the fable according to which he fled ʿUyayna as a result of having murdered its ruler, Ibn Muʿammar, in the mosque became a fact to a contemporary British consular report.[8] The incomprehension and misinformation in which Wahhabism was and is still engulfed is due to more than the fact that its works were little known outside Arabia (with the exception of India) until well into this century,[9] and certainly to more than the undoubted intellectual poverty and aridity of such works or to the relative isolation of Najd. The anti-Wahhabite polemic[10] was due principally to a primary and original trait of the Wahhabite movement and its concomitant ideology: that of making an absolute demarcation between an expanding polity and all its surroundings.

The social and political dimension of Wahhabite ideology is the setting of strict limits of exclusivity to a particular *ʿaṣabiyya* (tribal power group), thus rendering all that is external to this expanding *ʿaṣabiyya* social, political and geographical territory whose plunder and subjugation are legitimate, indeed incumbent upon members of this exclusive group.[11] *Kufr* (unbelief) is an attribute of others and, in the accentuated Wahhabite form, of otherness *tout court.* It is an attribute which makes conquest and subjugation incumbent, under the banner of *jihād*, both as the political act of an expanding polity and as a legal–religious obligation. This exterior of *kufr* comprises not only idolatrous religions, nor is it confined to non-Islamic monotheism, but describes non-Wahhabite co-religionists as well. Ibn ʿAbd al-Wahhāb himself emphasized this, justifying it on the analogy of Muḥammad himself having fought believers in the one God.[12] The hallowed principle of Sunnī Islam, according to which all those who profess the *shahāda* are Muslims, is rejected in favour of the assertion often made by Wahhabite divines that even reserve towards the necessity of pronouncing non-Wahhabites (generically dubbed *mushrikūn*) to be *kuffār* (unbelievers) and of fighting them in itself constitutes *kufr.*[13] Sulaymān b. ʿAbdillāh b. Muḥammad b. ʿAbd al-Wahhāb, a prominent grandson of the movement's founder, banned not only alliance with the *kuffār*, but also their employment, consultation, trust, visiting, advice, friendship, emulation, cordiality and affability towards them.[14] Needless to say, the full rigour of these principles was not always brought to bear; this was dependent on the political and social conditions of the time. The third Saudi *Imām*, Suʿud b. ʿAbd al-ʿAzīz b. Muḥammad, was particularly noted for his severity,[15] while the population of Qaṣīm in the north of Najd and their local divines were known for their relative leniency and considered neither the Ottomans nor other Muslims generally to be *kuffār*.

In the first instance, the concrete manifestation of otherness to be suppressed was the particular Najdī forms of *shirk*. This comprised such matters as the idol Dhā 'l-Khilṣa, destroyed very early in the history of Wahhabism,[16] against which apparently infertile women rubbed their buttocks in the hope of fertility[17] – Dhā 'l-khilṣa was the name of an idol destroyed in early Islamic times in Najd; it is not clear if what was involved in the eighteenth century was more than some sort of ritual re-enactment of this, made possible by the metonymical conflation of past and present in which fundamentalist discourse is grounded. Najdī *shirk* also involved the sanctification of the dead and supplication and sacrifice at their shrines, such as that of Zaynab bint al-Khaṭṭāb at Jubayla, where people sought success in business, or the cult of the male palm tree, at Bulaydat al-Fiḍḍa and elsewhere, to which spinsters flocked praying for matrimony, and much else.[18] The felling of sacred trees and the destruction of shrines (not the obliteration of graves or their desecration) were some of the very first acts of Ibn ʿAbd al-Wahhāb, who was particularly vehement in his condemnation of devotional acts directed towards any objects of sanctity other than God; these included supplication to the *jinn*, the celebration of feasts connected with the birth of persons of sacred attributes (including that of the Prophet himself), the use of talismans and of sorcery, and similar actions imputing potency to mere creatures.[19] Some of the first acts of the Wahhabite forces of Suʿūd b. ʿAbd al-Azīz upon the invasions of Mecca in 1803 and Medina in 1805 were the destruction of sacred domes designating shrines.[20] Over a century later, the Saudi government destroyed the dome of a shrine in Jidda supposedly containing the remains of Eve, and banned popular devotions at the site.[21] To these local iniquities were added others derived from conditions farther afield. One prominent Wahhabite divine in 1808 included among iniquitous practices in Syria the drinking of alcohol, the smoking of tobacco, the playing of cards and listening to popular story-tellers.[22] Finally, Shiʿite Muslims throughout the history of Wahhabism and until the establishment of Saudi Arabia have been a favoured target of unremitting Wahhābī ferocity, ideological as well as military; the Ismāʿīlī Shiʿites of the Banū Yām in ʿAsīr were eventually converted.

There can be little doubt that the Wahhabite assault on popular practices and on other manifestations of devotional and doctrinal difference was directed not only against dogmatic and devotional aberrations, but was also the counterpart of the fact that these were not only aberrant, but also and decidedly local. This acted to fragment religious authority in this world as well as in others, and militated against the emergence of a political authority which, busily devouring and incorporating social and geographical territory into a unifying vortex, was sustained by the Saudi–Wahhabite alliance.[23] Prior to the emergence of the Wahhabite state of the Suʿūd family, scholarly activity in Najd was scanty, although it was on the increase along with the growth in population in general, and urbanized habitation in particular, during the seventeenth century.[24] Much of this learning was cultivated in the context of connections with Damascus and (to a smaller degree) other centres where Hanbalism was in currency; indeed, the *adhān* in Burayda in the early part of this century was described by one observer as having been delivered in the tones of Syria.[25] Ibn ʿAbd al-Wahhāb himself belonged to a prominent scholarly family, and his twenty or so marriages,[26] some to members of the princely families of Muʿammar and Suʿūd, indicate social alliances concomitant with the politico-religious alliance in which his career and those of his descendants find their bearings.[27]

The role of Wahhābī divines is inseparable from the role of Wahhabite doctrine and its emphasis on the application of Islamic law; aspects of this will be analysed further below. The most direct aspect of the social alliance between divines and Saudi princes is the direct political role of the former. Though it may be true that the original compact between Muḥammad b. ʿAbd al-Wahhāb and Muḥammad b. Suʿūd at Dirʿiyya, the first Saudi capital, was one in which the divine was "the senior partner",[28] this is only so in the sense that it was he who was in charge of the legal system. Yet the pre-eminence of the Āl al-Shaykh, the descendants of Ibn ʿAbd al-Wahhāb, in the legal and religious institutions of successive Saudi states is a factor connected both with their position in family alliances and their capacity formally to charter transfers of power.[29] Acting upon the hallowed principle repeated by Ibn ʿAbd al-Wahhāb, that power is legitimate however it may have been seized, and that obedience to whoever wields this power is incumbent upon all his subjects – so much so that the prerogatives of the Imamate belong to the holder of power irrespective of his own status[30] – the senior ranks of the Wahhabite devotional and legal institutions have acted as legitimizers of the successive transitions of power within the House of Suʿūd, both peaceful and seditious. It appears that, in all cases, such legitimation, *bayʿa*, was always undertaken at the behest or command of the effective ruler.[31] In the period of turmoil and internecine Saudi struggle in the 1860s and 1870s which saw eight changes of supreme Saudi authority in Riyadh between the death of Fayṣal b. Turkī in 1865 and 1877, the position of the Wahhabite hierarchy embodied in Āl al-Shaykh was one of attempts to reconcile, followed by the recognition of the victorious party.[32]

The Āl al-Shaykh have therefore been rather like the house clerics of the Saudi clan, to whom their loyalty never wavered even in the worst days of Egyptian occupation in the early nineteenth century or during the ascendancy of the Āl Rashīd of Ḥāʾil. For leadership in the desert polity, which the Saudi states were, was the prerogative of a particular clan within a possible wider federation, and this polity was based on the absolute pre-eminence of a particular family combined with the political peripheralization of others. As always, desert polity is based on the patrimonial ascendancy of a particular clan – here the Suʿūds – which holds in tow an alliance of other clans which are by definition tributary and excluded from power. And whereas the leading clan – the only one, strictly speaking, which can arrogate to itself a political role – does not base its emergence to leadership on the extraction of public surplus but derives its wealth from private property and trade, its role as political leader, and the geographical expansion of this role, is based on systematic utilization of public surplus, a fact which is made possible by the tributarization of subject populations.[33] A similar situation, that of the Rashīdī state at Ḥāʾil, has been described in an excellent account as a trade state at the core, and a tribute state at the periphery,[34] and one could well say the same about the successive Saudi states. Built upon the settled population of al-ʿĀriḍ (the early Islamic Yamāma), it came to command and extract surplus from the trade of Qaṣīm, whose rival towns of Burayda and ʿUnayza sat astride the important Baṣra–Medina route and held one of the key routes to Kuwait; others to Kuwait and Bahrain passed in more southerly territory. These territories were early incorporated into the Saudi state, although they seem to have been prepared readily to turn against it in times of crisis, as during the Egyptian intervention.[35] From the Gulf Najdī trade reached as far as India, and ʿUnayza traders had a stake in a pearling trade whose main buying organization was, in the early part of this century, represented by an M. Rosenthal of Paris, known locally as Ḥabīb.[36] Besides trade in necessities, the export of horses was sometimes significant and sometimes in decline.[37] Also in the territorial core of Wahhabite polity was an erratic, but sometimes flourishing, agriculture.[38]

The bedouin tribes, however, were connected with this system only in so far as trade routes passed through their territory, *dīra*, and from this passage they extracted protection fees and offered guidance services. The ʿAjmān, for instance, controlled routes between Najd and both Kuwait and Ḥasā. Similarly, other tribes of the surrounding territories, such as ʿUtayba, Āl Murra, Muṭayr, ʿAniza (to which the House of Suʿūd "belong"), Shammar, and others, controlled routes leading to other territories, the Ḥijāz, Syria, and elsewhere. But for these tribes to come to be considered as anything other than idolators, they had to be incorporated into the political system whose core was (and still is) the Saudi clan. This entailed these tribes becoming tributaries to the centre of power in southern Najd, and this, in its turn, entailed not only their subjection to taxation (in kind such as camels), but also their exclusion from the political sphere. The centralization in the extraction of surplus and the elimination of the role of these nomadic tribes in the extraction of surplus for their own benefit, as they did from protection fees (*khuwwa*) paid by agriculturalists and by traders passing through tribal territories, implied more than the technical reorganization of such extraction in general by relegating this task to a central authority which then redistributed to every group its proper due. It also implied political eradication, that is, the abrogation of tribal right for the benefit of a political right exclusively exercised by the centre. This new political right erected over the debris of tribal right is itself derived from an eminently tribal concept, that of protection, *ḥimāya*, exercised by the central authority,[39] in exactly the same way as the nomadic tribes had hitherto offered protection and thus politically neutralized settled and trading groups in return for taxation. The relation of power expressed in its exercise, and thus the exercise of politics, by certain groups, and the exclusion of others from it, is the means by which tribal society is stratified. This selfsame process is repeated, in reverse, in the subjugation of nomadic tribes to the centre.[40]

Martial nomadism is thus emasculated by its reduction to the same vulnerability and susceptibility to fiscal subjugation, with its concomitant political obliteration, that had been the lot of the weaker agricultural settlements. In the religious terms of Wahhabite divines and of the principles of government they imparted to the House of Suʿūd, this reduction of nomads, agriculturalists and townspeople equally into subjects of the Saudi polity, this compact of protection and allegiance, was expressed in terms of the canonical alms tax, the *zakāt*.[41] Religious ordinances advocated by reformists are never disembodied, and their practical translation in the Wahhabite instance is a compact of protection between unequal parties modelled on tribal relations. The one is unthinkable without the other. It appears that the Saudi clan, by means of the military forces it could muster from the ʿĀriḍī population and its own domestic militia (*fidāwiyya, zghurtiyya*), and by skilful manipulation of desert and international diplomacy, not to speak of the use of vast wealth accruing from agriculture, trade, and various forms of tribute, was capable of turning itself into the only unit in the territory of faith which plays the role hitherto performed by martial nomadic tribes; the erstwhile masters of the desert are thus transformed into tribal tributaries connected to the House of Suʿūd by ties of obligation brought about by unequal power. That is why the founder of Saudi Arabia invoked ties of kinship with tribal groups way out of his areas of control to express his bid for expansion.[42]

With the *zakāt* the criterion of inclusion within the exclusive group is indicated; the group comprises the parties to a compact of unequal power, sharing a common exterior which exists for the purpose of expansion. The incursions of Wahhabite forces in Iraq, Syria, the Ḥijāz, the Yemen and Oman in the early nineteenth and early twentieth centuries are instances of this. War being one vital manner in which tribal groups cohere, it is clearly impossible effectively to detribalize tribes and to atomize tribesmen by means of subjection to *zakāt* and simultaneously to have them as tribal units with a tributary status; the only effective solution to this was agricultural settlement and the physical obliteration of tribal military force, both of which ʿAbd al-ʿAzīz was to attempt in the first third of this century, succeeding in the second.[43]

Zakāt is only one manifestation, albeit one of great importance, of the tendency of Wahhabism to homogenize that society subject to the control of the House of Suʿūd. *Sharʿ*, of which *zakāt* is an instance, is certainly the method whereby society is homogenized, rid of its irregularity and reconstituted so that it becomes more amenable to central direction. *Lex talionis* was one thing that the *sharʿ* imposed by Wahhabism on both nomads and townspeople abolished; it prescribed the substitution of money for blood, but this worked imperfectly,[44] indicating an as yet unconsummated project. The prohibition of usury, widely used amongst the bedouin,[45] is a similar issue. Customary marriage not involving a proper Muslim contract, and the customary division of inheritance whereby women were deprived of canonical shares, were common practice, particularly among bedouins,[46] who in some cases favoured the marriage of women who were already married but whose husbands were in captivity.[47] It was not until Saudi power was consolidated by means of *zakāt*-collecting local agents that the *sharʿ* and precepts derived from it were applied by the legal authorities answerable to the Wahhabite divines.[48] Just as local devotions detracted from the authority of the centre, so did local customs for which there was the possibility of a central provision that could be enforced by the corps of Wahhabite '*ulamā*'. In all cases, Wahhabism in its devotional as well as its legal aspects seems an element for the homogenization of society.

But this homogenization had limits that we have already touched upon, namely, the fact that domination of the tributary type exercised by tribal polity based on the absolute monopoly of power by one particular clan requires the maintenance of tribal particularism and of the social system of stratification prevalent in the desert. Homogenization is a political, not necessarily a social, process. It is thus not surprising that, despite the vehemence of Wahhabite proselytism, the Ṣulubba were untouched by it, although they did not dwell *in partibus infidelium* but nevertheless revered the stars and held beliefs akin to heathens.[49] But this finds its explanation in their caste-like social inferiority and occupational stratification. Conversely, status and political necessity were allowed to override the requirements of the *sharʿ* in cases of personal status touching princely or royal personalities. The frequent marriages of members of the Suʿūd clan, in some instances for no more than one or two nights, are sometimes reminiscent of Shiʿite *mutʿa* marriage, proscribed by all legal schools of Sunnī Islam.[50] Particularity could not be eliminated as totally as Wahhabite doctrine might require, and it is undoubtedly true that the ethos of Wahhabism, with its embeddedness in tribal society, militated against the very homogenization it prescribed and required for its total practical consummation. This is why the administration of legal as opposed to customary justice, especially the attempts to eliminate the right of asylum and blood revenge, was at best very imperfect and had to await the modern Saudi state for its serious implementation.[51] It is according to this contextual condition, or reality principle, of Wahhabite fundamentalism that Wahhabite polity, with the definitive establishment of the state in the first quarter of the twentieth century, becomes strictly Saudi polity. Saudi polity tributarizes other clan groups no longer nomadic, and ties them as clans stratified according to a particular pecking order to the redistribution of Saudi wealth; for plunder is substituted subsidy and the privileges of citizenship, such as the legal sponsorship of foreign business (*kafāla*), akin in many ways to the exaction of protection money (*khuwwa*). Thus tribalism becomes ascendant, not merely a *modus vivendi* or a traditional structure of society. For its part, Wahhabism abstains willy-nilly from ordering society, and becomes a state ideology in the most common acceptation of "ideology". Wahhabism remains pervasive not only in the educational system, the media, and public discourse in general, but also in international proselytizing and other activities, not to speak of its spectacular performances in the shape of the public punishment of errants and criminals, much reminiscent of the Roman circus. Indeed, the Saudi–Wahhabite alliance reminds one of one Roman principle of statecraft, *panis et circenses.*

Yet Wahhabism preserves its integrity entire. For despite complications of unwieldy reality, Wahhabism sought the abstraction of society according to a utopian model whose current name is "fundamentalism", denoting the attempt to fashion society according to a fundamental model already accomplished. Like all fundamentalism, Wahhabite doctrine[52] is cast in the mode of revivification. It purports to detail the exemplary behaviour of the Prophet and his contemporaries, and to utilize this register of exemplaries as a charter for reform. The fundamentals of rectitude are contained in this register, and the history that intervenes between the occurrence of exemplary acts and today is an accident that no more than sullies and corrupts its origin, and which therefore can be eliminated, as history is the mere passage of time, not the work of social, political and cultural transformations. It is not chance or an act of incomprehensible blindness to the facts of history that causes the fundamental doctrinal texts of the Wahhabite movement – Ibn ʿAbd al-Wahhāb's *Kitāb al-Tawḥīd* and its main commentaries and glosses[53] – to contain little concrete reference to contemporary reality, but to be rather like commentaries on this reality in a different medium, that of detailing exemplary acts and sayings culled from historical and scriptural knowledge. The two are set in parallel registers and are expressed in terms of today's fundamentally right bearings, making the iniquities of today less historical realities than supervening mistakes which can be eliminated by reference to exemplary precedent.

History is therefore reversible; alternatively, that history which interjects itself between the fundamental examples of the past and today is liable to elimination. Wahhabite doctrine not being historical scholarship, this position finds its bearings in the social and political being of this doctrine. For the import of fundamentalism is to require its (willing or unwilling) adherents to become subject to its requirements, that is, to lay Wahhabite territory open to the authority of Wahhabism, and therefore subject to the Saudi polity. By requiring subjection in principle to the authority whose voice is Wahhabism, this doctrine simultaneously renders these subjects open to the dictation of cultural and societal relations whose ground and condition are this authority. In short, Wahhabite fundamentalism puts forward a model whose task is to subject local societies with their customs, authorities, devotions, and other particularities to a general process of acculturation[54] which prepares them for membership in the commonwealth whose linchpin and exclusive *raison d'être* is the absolute dominance of the House of Suʿūd.

Such is the import of the abstraction from contemporary reality which marks all fundamentalism: an absence is engendered, which is filled by interpretations provided by those with the means of enforcing an interpretation. It leaves the way open for the social and political contexts of fundamentalist doctrine to weave themselves into the terms of fundamentalist discourse, and by so doing to translate the terms of this discourse into contemporary facts and realities. The abstract reference of Wahhabite ideology has its counterpart also in the infinite possibilities for endowing it with meaning by those capable of enforcing a particular interpretation. The major one in this context is the abstract exterior, open for correction and demanding of struggle: instead of local and other infidels, the spectre of communism is posited by the Saudi state, autonomously and in tandem with its almost utter dependence on the United States, as the primary evil and manifestation of *kufr* and *shirk*. Fact and fantasy become tokens of each other. Wahhabism thus seeks to flatten the contours of societies under its authority and to prepare them for the receipt of new form by those powers who wield the ultimate authority and the ultimate sanction of force – the House of Su ʿūd. Thus the definition of the interior in terms dictated by political authorities is the counterpart of the iniquitous exterior defined by the divines of Wahhabite doctrine.

The definition of this interior is based on the fundamentalist mode of perceiving this interior, in the sense that presentation of the present in terms of scriptural and historical examples eliminates its reality and transforms it into a *tabula rasa* on which the authoritarian writ can be inscribed. This is the import of the execration of *taqlīd* from the days of Ibn ʿAbd al-Wahhāb,[55] in line with a long Hanbalite tradition. And since law perhaps best reflects the transformations of reality, it is there that the encounter between Wahhabite doctrine and the political and social reality for which it is the charter is best regarded; the legal system of the Saudi state is based on the twin pillars of devotional severity, whose ultimate authority is the Koran and the *sunna* as mediated by the authority of Wahhabism and its professionals (imams, *muṭawwiʿ* corps), and of legal liberalism, one of whose most important categories is that of public welfare or the common weal, *maṣlaḥa*.[56] The liberalism of the Saudi legal system is not only manifested in the wide use of discretionary legislation based on the notion of *maṣlaḥa*, in line with Hanbalite tradition, but in a strong tendency towards doctrinal eclecticism, and the wise use of non-Hanbalite law,[57] particularly after 1961.[58] All in all, economic legislation is Saudi Arabia has been consonant with conditions prevalent there. "Islamic banking", for instance, is consonant with conditions of speculative capitalism such as exist in Arabia today, and is in many ways reminiscent of European banking practices in the early nineteenth century.

Maṣlaḥa and devotional puritanism therefore become the twin pillars of the construction of the Wahhabite interior,[59] and both have the sanction of Wahhabism and its professionals. The king's prerogative as imam in the conduct of politics according to the *sharʿ*

becomes referred to as *ijtihād*.[60] Thus when a *fatwā* pronounced the insurance of commercial goods to be illegal, King ʿAbd al-ʿAzīz reversed the ruling on the grounds of public interest.[61] And when the Wahhabite divines wanted to abolish the commercial codes of the Ḥijāz which had been modelled on the Ottoman *Mejelle*, ʿAbd al-ʿAzīz desisted and, when this code was overhauled in 1931, it was simply purged of reference to interest and was still modelled on the Ottoman code of 1850.[62] The king's position was clear from the outset. He declared publicly that he would abide by the judgements of Ibn ʿAbd al-Wahhāb and others only if they were demonstrable with reference to the scriptures;[63] direct reference to scriptures with the elimination of intervening authorities implies *ipso facto* a call for reinterpretation. Such is the real import of the rejection of *taqlīd* and the injunction to *ijtihād*.

The Saudi–Wahhabite alliance therefore subjected populations to legal abstraction, cleared the way for legislation in line with the discretionary requirements of what is habitually termed "development", and inflicted upon these populations a constant social invigilation and control undertaken by the corps of *muṭawwiʿūn* who assure adherence to standard devotions and precepts of public puritanism. This last function assures the control over social relations that obtain in the tribal society which Saudi polity has always considered to be its natural domain, relations that entail the strict exclusion of women, the observance of very conservative attitudes, and other means of severe social control, in addition to rituals of inwardness, such as public punishments. Such puritanism has often been the counterpart of economic liberalism, and Saudi Arabia is no exception. Yet the constraints on tribalism as well as on the consummation of a strict and integral Wahhabite order, both the results of practical Wahhabism, have resulted in two major episodes that have disturbed the Saudi–Wahhabite order.

The first was the series of events which led to the final military elimination of the Ikhwān during the late 1920s. These were irregular forces levied from settlements of bedouin populations known as the *hujar*, modelled on the *hijra* of Muḥammad and designed as places of exemplary life and repositories of military manpower at the disposal of the Saudi state, and established from about 1908 onwards at various strategic locations in Najd on tribal territories belonging to the clans.[64] They were therefore tribal-military settlements, extensively subsidized by ʿAbd al-ʿAzīz,[65] and marked by the observance of strict codes of fundamentalist morality, including a vestimentary code.[66]

ʿAbd al-ʿAzīz did not construct a civic militia in the *hujar* – he had his townsmen for this purpose – but constructed tribal abodes with definable boundaries. We have seen that the Wahhabite–Saudi alliance deprives social collectivities of a political constitution, but preserves them as social units. This applies especially to nomadic tribal groups, which sustained their social being by raids into infidel territory, not only for booty, but for the maintenance of desert social stratification, as has already been suggested. When the borders of present-day Saudi Arabia were solidifying as a result of agreements and treaties, mainly with Great Britain, the checks put on bedouin raiding activity led to a situation expressed by one of the leaders of the Ikhwān revolt, Fayṣal al-Duwaysh, chief of the Muṭayr and of the Arṭawiyya *hijra*, as one in which "we are neither Moslems fighting the unbelievers nor are we Arabs and Bedouins raiding each other and living on what we get from each other".[67] The Ikhwān had indeed "worked themselves out of a job",[68] and a conflagration was inevitable and was predicted by a discerning ethnologist.[69]

The exterior was no longer to be territory open to conquest and subjection, as it should be with Wahhabite doctrine, and the revolt of the Ikhwān might have turned into a general rebellion had it not been for the fact that an analogue of external plunder was found: oil, the wealth accruing from which is redistributed after a patrimonial manner according to the pecking order required by, and conducive to, the maintenance of tribal structures and status. The distinctions brought about by wealth and privilege, the correlatives of the tribal structure, define a novel exterior, that of expatriates employed in Saudi Arabia, over and above the local exterior, women.

So much for the disturbing social consequences of Wahhabite polity. As for the ideological consequences of this polity, that is, of the Wahhabite–Saudi alliance, these have taken a form unchanged since 1927 when the Ikhwān, in full rebellion, charged ʿAbd al-ʿAzīz with violating the relationship of interior and exterior by sending his son Suʿūd to Egypt (occupied by a Christian power and inhabited by infidel Muslims), using wireless telegraphy and other works of the devil, not compelling the Shiʿites of Ḥasā to adopt the Wahhabite creed, and so forth.[70] Indeed, the Ikhwān had been suspicious of ʿAbd al-ʿAzīz's dealings with infidels from a much earlier date; in 1918 they were not enthusiastic about the campaign against the

Wahhabite Ḥāʾil, on the assumption that they were playing a British political game.[71] Very much the same sort of objection to the political power of the Saudi state was voiced by the participants in the seizure of the Great Mosque with the Kaʿba at Mecca in November 1979 – the second episode to disturb the Saudi–Wahhabite order. One chief iniquity and manifestation of *kufr* is the constant contact and co-operation with Christians; and the state which pretends to *tawḥīd*, the technical name of Wahhabism, in fact performed the unification, *tawḥīd*, between Muslims, Christians and polytheists, confirmed Shʿites in their heresies, and, while it combated fetishism, instituted the fetish of money.[72] The facts of today, in perfectly fundamentalist manner, are assimilated to scripturalist models and are made to translate them, and the prime motif of the group which precipitated the events of 1979 was the assimilation of contemporary events to eschatological events,[73] which justified their messianic revolt.

The Wahhabite divines who condemned the 1979 rebels to death[74] are truer representatives of Wahhabism than the dead puritans. The grand Muftī of Saudi Arabia, Shaykh ʿAbd al-ʿAzīz b. Bāz, a signatory to the death sentence,[75] did not seem to disagree with the theses of the rebels who had read some of their treatises to him, but simply declined to specify the object of criticism as the present Saudi state.[76] The secret of fundamentalism resides in the absence of specification, in the very tokenism of the letter, in the parallelism but never in the identity of the scriptural and the real registers. The latter can therefore be the meaning of the former through the imputation of such meaning by the agency that has the power and authority to posit, consolidate, and enforce meaning. The impossibility of utopia derives from the impossibility of conflating the two registers and contexts of reference, the scriptural and the real. Juhaymān al-ʿUtaybī and his followers conflated the two registers and identified them. They consequently read the eschatological script as an immanent chiliasm, precipitating their mundane perdition. Without the distinction between the registers which allows the powers that be to penetrate the script and infuse it with their power, fundamentalism becomes redundant, an idle chiliasm without a chance in this world.

Notes

1. I use this term in preference to *Muwaḥḥidūn* used by the Wahhabites because it is common and because the latter is confusing, being used by the Druze and, indeed, by all Muslims, to designate themselves.

2. M.Sh. Alūsī, *Tārīkh Najd* [History of Najd], ed. M.B. Atharī, Cairo, AH 1343; AD 1924, p. 50.

3. Ibid., pp. 50ff.

4. For instance, Al-Jabartī, *Min Akhbār al-Hijāz wa Najd fī Tārīkh al-Jabartī* [Narratives on Hijaz and Najd from the History of Jabartī], ed. M.A. Ghālib, n.p. 1975, p. 97.

5. H. Khalaf al-Shaykh Khazʿal, *Ḥayāt al-Shaykh Muḥammad b. ʿAbd al-Wahhāb*, Beirut 1968, pp. 119ff.

6. Fleischer (trans.), "Briefwechsel zwischen den Anführender Wahhabiten und dem Paša von Damascus", *Zeitschrift der Deutschen Morgenländischen Gesellschaft*, xi, 1857, p. 441.

7. Ibn Bishr, *ʿUnwān al-Majd fī Tārīkh Najd* [Summits of Glory in the History of Najd], 2 vols, Riyadh AH 1385, 1388; AD 1965, 1968, vol. 1, p. 18.

8. M.A. Khan, "A Diplomat's Report on Wahhabism in Arabia", *Islamic Studies*, 7, 1968, p. 40.

9. M. Kurd ʿAlī, *Al-Qadīm wa 'l-Ḥadīth* [The Classical and the Modern], Cairo 1925, p. 157.

10. See M.R. Riḍā, *Al-Wahhābiyya wa 'l-Ḥijāz* [Wahhabism and the Hijāz], Cairo AH 1344; AD 1925, for a critical exposition, and see in general Z.I. Karout, "Anti-wahhabitische Polemik im XIX. Jahrhundert", unpublished doctoral dissertation, University of Bonn, 1978.

11. The best account of the social and political bearings of Wahhabite ideology and of the overall history of the movement is that of W. Sharāra, *Al-Ahl wa 'l-Ghanīma: Muqawwimāt al-Siyāsa fī 'l-Mamlaka al-ʿArabiyya al-Suʿūdiyya* [Clansmen and Booty: The Principles of Politics in the Saudi Arabian Kingdom], Beirut 1981.

12. *Majmuʿat al-Tawḥīd*, Saudi Arabia n.d., p. 52 and passim.

13. Ibid., pp. 284 and passim.

14. Ibid., pp. 121–2 and cf. pp. 251ff., 288–9, 292.

15. Alūsī, *Tārīkh Najd*, p. 94.

16. H. Wahba, *Arabian Days*, London 1964, pp. 99 and 112.

17. Ibn Bishr, *ʿUnwān al-Majd*, vol. 1, p. 6.

18. Wahba, *Arabian Days*, p. 87.

19. For instance, Ibn ʿAbd al-Wahhāb, in *Majmūʿat al-Tawḥīd* [The Tawhid Collection], pp. 9–10, 58, 66 and passim.

20. Jabartī, *Akhbār al-Ḥijāz*, pp. 92, 104.

21. H. Wahba, *Jazīrat al-ʿArab fī'l-Qarn al-ʿIshrīn* [The Arabian Peninsula in the Twentieth Century], Cairo 1967, p. 31. For practices of talismans and magical healing in today's Ḥijāz, see M. Katakura, *Bedouin*

Village. A Study of a Saudi Arabian People in Transition, Tokyo 1977, pp. 68–9.

22. Fleischer, "Briefwechsel", p. 438.

23. Sharāra, *Al-Ahl wa'l-Ghanīma*, p. 91.

24. U.M. Al-Juhany, "The History of Najd prior to the Wahhabis. A Study of the Social, Political and Religious Conditions in Najd during Three Centuries", unpublished PhD Thesis, University of Washington, 1983, pp. 250ff. On population, see pp. 165ff. It must be stressed that Juhany's conclusions are based on sketchy source material and that they should be treated with some caution as indicating general trends rather than anything else.

25. H. St.John B. Philby, *Arabia of the Wahhabis*, London 1977, repr. from 1928 edn, p. 195.

26. Khalaf al-Shaykh Khazʿal, *Ḥayāt al-Shaykh Muḥammad b. ʿAbd al-Wahhāb*, p. 341.

27. Ibn ʿAbd al-Wahhāb's sworn and active enemy was his own brother (ibid., pp. 250ff).

28. M.J. Crawford, 'Wahhābī *ʿulamā*' and the Law, 1745–1932', unpublished M.Phil thesis, University of Oxford, 1980, p. 38.

29. Ibid., pp. 42ff., 52.

30. Khalaf al-Shaykh Khazʿal, *Ḥayāt al-Shaykh Muḥammad b. ʿAbd al-Wahhāb*, p. 140.

31. For instance, Ibn Bishr, *ʿUnwān al-Majd*, vol. 1, pp. 96, 101, 203; vol. 2, p. 60.

32. See the discussion of this by M.J. Crawford, "Civil War, Foreign Intervention and the Question of Political Legitimacy: A Nineteenth-Century Saʿūdī Qāḍī's Dilemma", *International Journal of Middle East Studies*, 14, 1982, pp. 227ff.

33. For the stratification of Najdī society, see Juhany, "History of Najd", pp. 173ff.

34. H. Rosenthal, "The Social Composition of the Military in the Process of State Formation in the Arabian Desert", *Journal of the Royal Anthropological Institute*, 95, 1965, pp. 184ff and passim.

35. Ibn Bishr, *ʿUnwān al-Majd*, vol. 1, p. 240.

36. Philby, *Arabia of the Wahhabis*, p. 285.

37. For instance, R.B. Winder, *Saudi Arabia in the Nineteenth Century*, London 1965, p. 214; J.G. Lorimer, *Gazetteer of the Persian Gulf, 'Omān and Central Arabia*, 6 vols, Calcutta 1908–15, vol. 1, pt. 2, pp. 2335ff; Philby, *Arabia of the Wahhabis*, p. 216.

38. For a full description of the earlier period, see Juhany, "History of Najd", pp. 182ff.

39. Cf. Sharāra, *Al-Ahl wa'l-Ghanīma*, p. 67.

40. On the Saudi taxation system, see, for instance, Winder, *Saudi Arabia*, pp. 211ff.

41. Cf. C.M. Helms, *The Cohesion of Saudi Arabia*, London 1981, pp. 152ff.

42. Kh. Ziriklī, *Shibh Jazīrat al-ʿArab fī ʿAhd al-Malik ʿAbd al-ʿAzīz* [The Arabian Peninsula under King Abd al-ʿAzīz], Beirut 1970, p. 290; and A. Rihani, *Maker of Modern Arabia*, Boston and New York 1928, pp. 60–61.

43. See the detailed account of J.S. Habib, *Ibn Saud's Warriors of Islam. The Ikhwan of Najd and their Role in the Creation of the Saʿudi Kingdom, 1910–1930*, Leiden 1978.

44. For instance, Winder, *Saudi Arabia*, pp. 158–9.

45. J.L. Burckhardt, *Notes on the Bedouins and the Wahábys*, London 1831, vol. 2, p. 150.

46. Ibid., vol. 1, pp. 107, 131; J. Chelhod, *Le Droit dans la société bédouine*, Paris 1971, pp. 70–71, 134; J. Henninger, "Das Eigentumsrecht bei den heutigen Beduinen Arabiens", *Zeitschrift für vergleichende Rechtswissenschaft*, 61, 1959, p. 29.

47. Ziriklī, *Shibh Jazīrat alʿArab*, p. 464.

48. For instance, Burckhardt, *Bedouins and the Wahábys*, vol. 1, pp. 99, 101, 120; vol. 2, pp. 136–9.

49. For a description, see Lewis Pelly, *Journal of a Journey from Persia to India through Herat and Candahar. By Lieut. Colonel Lewis Pelly . . . also Report of a Journey to the Wahabee Capital of Riyadh in Central Arabia.* Bombay 1866, pp. 189ff.

50. One could also cite as evidence of animist manifestations (or survivals) the *wasm* with which ʿAbd al-ʿAzīz branded his camels, described by Philby, *Arabia of the Wahhabis*, p. 53, and sketched in H.R.P. Dickson, *The Arab of the Desert*, London 1949, p. 420.

51. Cf. for instance Winder, *Saudi Arabia*, p. 208.

52. A thorough sketch can be found in H. Laoust, *Essai sur les doctrines morales et politiques de Takī-d-Dīn Aḥmad b. Taimīya*, Cairo 1939, bk 3, ch. 2.

53. Sulaymān b. ʿAbdillāh b. Muḥammad b. ʿAbd al-Wahhāb's *Taysīr al-ʿAzīz al-Ḥamīd fī Sharḥ Kitāb al-Tawḥīd*, Damascus n.d. [1962], is a detailed linguistic and historical commentary; *Fatḥ al-Majīd* by ʿAbd al-Raḥmān b. Ḥasan Āl al-Shaykh, Riyadh n.d., is in many ways a summary of its predecessor, while the same author's *Qurrat ʿUyūn al-Muwaḥḥidīn fī Taḥqīq Daʿwat al-Anbiyāʾ al-Mursalīn*, Riyadh n.d., is a collection of glosses on the original.

54. Cf. Sharāra, *Al-Ahl wa'l-Ghanīma*, p. 101.

55. Text in *Majmūʿat al-Tawḥīd*, p. 60.

56. See, for instance, Crawford, "Wahhābī *ʿulamāʾ*", pp. 68, 110.

57. For instance, ibid., pp. 70–71.

58. A.W.I. Abu Sulaiman, *The Role of Ibn Qudāma in Ḥanbalī Jurisprudence*, unpublished PhD thesis, University of London, 1970, p. 248.

59. Cf. O. Carré, "Idéologie et pouvoir en Arabie Saoudite et dans son entourage", in P. Bonnenfant, ed., *La Péninsule arabique d'aujourdhui*, Paris 1982, vol. 1, pp. 242–3 and passim.

60. Crawford, "Wahhābī *ʿulamāʾ*", p. 111.

61. Wahba, *Arabian Days*, p. 94.

62. Crawford, "Wahhābī *ʿulamāʾ*", p. 97; Wahba, *Jazīrat al-ʿArab*, pp. 319ff.

63. A. Rīḥānī, *Tārīkh Najd al-Ḥadīth* [The Modern History of Najd], vol. 5 of Rīḥānī, *Al-Aʿmāl al-ʿArabiyya al-Kāmila* [Complete Arabic Works], Beirut 1980, p. 374.

64. A. Musil, *North Neğd. A Topographical Itinerary*, Oriental Explorations and Studies, no. 4, New York 1928, p. 283.

65. Habib, *Ibn Saud's Warriors*, p. 143.

66. Ibid., pp. 33ff.

67. Ibid., p. 136.

68. Ibid., p. 119.

69. Musil, *Northern Nejd*, p. 303.

70. Habib, *Ibn Saud's Warriors*, pp. 122, 135. On the curious controversy over telegraphy, see Wahba, *Arabian Days*, pp. 57–8.

71. Philby, *Arabia of the Wahhabis*, p. 102.

72. Juhaymān b. Muḥammad b. Sayf al-ʿUtaybī, *Daʿwat al-Ikhwān: Kayfa Badaʾat wa ilā ayn Tasīr* [The Call of the Ikhwān: How it Started and Where it is Heading], n.d., pp. 32–3; and *Al-Imāra wa ʾl-Bayʿa wa ʾl-Ṭāʿa wa Kashf Talbīs al-Ḥukkām ʿalā Ṭalabat al-ʿIlm wa ʾl-ʿAwāmm* [Rulership and Delegation of Power and Obedience and the Unveiling of Rulers' Shares against Commoners and Scholars] (n.p., n.d.), p. 28.

73. ʿUtaybī, *Al-Fitan wa Akhbār al-Mahdī wa ʾl-Dajjāl wa Nuzūl ʿĪsā b. Maryam wa Ashrāṭ al-Sāʿa* [Eschatological Disturbances and Narratives of the Messiah and Antichrist and the Descent of Jesus and Signs of the Apocalypse], n.d., passim; and *Al-Imāra*, pp. 20–21.

74. The text of this *fatwā* and other documentation is contained in ʿA. Maṭiʿnī, *Jarīmat al-ʿAṣr. Qiṣṣat Iḥtilāl al-Masjid al-Ḥarām* [The Crime of the Epoch. The Story of the Occupation of the Holy Mosque], Cairo 1980, pp. 43–4.

75. Ibid., p. 45.

76. ʿUtaybī, *Daʿwat al-Ikhwān*, p. 8.

7

Islamic Studies and the European Imagination

... quasi tota natura cum ipsis insaniret

Spinoza

It was customary for medieval Muslim scholars and divines to deliver a public lecture marking the translation to a professorship. The purpose of this rite of passage was not entirely ritual nor necessarily frivolous, and need not be so today. It gave the incumbent the chance publicly to announce the provenance of his learning, to declare the direction of his scholarship, to inventorize his stock-in-trade, and to scrutinize the state of his field. Such formal statement of scholarly patrimony and intent is salutary. Reflection is always creditable; and taking up a chair, like the mid-life crisis, is a good vantage point for reflection, and I am perhaps fortunate in that the two do not coincide in my case. Without reflection, scholarship will become and remain captive to the unaided native intelligence, the truest companion error, and of course prejudice: prejudice shared with one's fellow-professionals and with society at large.

I wish to continue this tradition; but I am acutely aware that an antique tradition such as this can only persist if subjected to change. So I shall invert the venerable order of things. I shall not assert the antiquity of my scientific pedigree. Neither do I propose to underline my faithfulness to my profession of orientalist, nor do I wish to celebrate what commonplace prejudices I might share with this profession and tradition. What I intend my reflections to do is to scrutinize the condition of my orientalist profession and patrimony, and perhaps to perform a metaphorical act of parricide. I will take up two interconnected matters. I shall first discuss the way in which a particular notion of Islam is conjured up by the European orientalist imagination and how this has provided and still provides Islamic studies as a scholarly discipline within orientalism with conceptual and categorical baggage which I repudiate.[1] Let me add here a word about orientalism: I understand by orientalism the deliberate apprehension and knowledge of the orient; I see orientalism as an ideological trope, an aesthetic, normative and ultimately political designation of things as oriental in opposition to occidental. It endows such things with changeless, "oriental" properties, some repellent and others charming, that go beyond history, that violate the changing nature of things, and that confirm them in a distant and irreducible specificity transcending the bounds of reason and forever valorizing common fantasy and folklore. To complement this first line of reflection, I shall briefly indicate major orientations for the dissolution of this orientalist category of Islam, and for the reconstitution of the study of Islam on the solid grounds of modern historical scholarship.

Let me first recall a predecessor, who to my knowledge was the first orientalist at Exeter. In 1704, Messrs Philip Bishop and Edward Score, of the High Street in Exeter, published a book entitled *A True and Faithful Account of the Religion and Manners of the Mohammedans.* The author, one Joseph Pitts, was born in Exeter. In 1678 at the age of seventeen, he fell victim to his king's rapacious activities in the Mediterranean, when the ship on which he served his apprenticeship was overwhelmed by Algerian corsairs. Nobody thought him worthy of a ransom, and he spent the next fifteen years in slavery, during which time he converted to Islam and made the pilgrimage to Mecca, but finally escaped and returned to spend the rest of his days in Exeter.

The book was quite a success; it went into at least four editions, and was reprinted in London as late as 1774; and this success was fully deserved, as the book almost completely confirmed the expectations of its readers, and there are strong indications that it was actually written according to printers' specifications. With the exception of such fantasies as could be falsified by tangible observation – such as the assertion of countless generations of Europeans that Muhammad's tomb in Medina was suspended in mid-air – the book rehearsed the usual repertoire of folkloristic absurdities current for centuries, absurdities which arise from a fundamental structure of all orientalist discourse: namely, that observations, and judgements without reference to observation, constitute two separate registers, with hardly any means of contact between the one and the other except for the possibility of the latter (judgements) given the guise of the former. Such are, of course, the possibilities of fantasy. Thus Islam was still for Pitts, as for medieval Europeans and a number of young orientalists today, "a miscellany of popery, Judaism, and the gentilism of the Arabs". The Turks – the quintessence of Islam for Pitts and his contemporaries – are so much given to sodomy that "they loath the Natural Use of the Woman" and Muhammad could be nothing but "a vile and debauch'd imposter". The Koran for Pitts, needless to say, is but "a Legend of Falsities, and abominable Follies and Absurdities".[2]

That observation is incapable of correcting prejudice was not a matter confined to semi-literate personalities such as Joseph Pitts. A still more staggering contrast is observable between Voltaire's nearly modern and historical view of Islam in his *Essai sur les moeurs*, and the dark medievalism of his tragedy, *Le Fanatisme ou Mahomet le Prophète.* That Muhammad was an imposter dominated by ambition and lust, and that he was therefore a worthy inspiration for Islam, is a medieval view which was shared by Edward Gibbon as by many until very recently. This medieval canon on Islam was fully formed by the end of the twelfth century, the offspring of two independent but remarkably parallel traditions of anti-Islamic polemic, the one Byzantine and the other Mozarabic. This canon, both theological and literary, was remarkably impervious to observation. Marco Polo's descriptions are largely based on literary and theological conventions which were astonishingly resistant to the observation of reality or to the reading of original Arabic sources, although these had already been available in translation from the time of the Cluniac collection in the middle of the twelfth century. And replete with factual information as they were, the medieval romances, the *histoire chanté* of the time, were yet unremitting in their subordination of fact to propaganda and literary convention. It appears that Crusaders and others who were in direct contact with Muslims learnt nothing about them, and only borrowed the arts of gracious living. For the rest, the Islamic orient was a source of fantasy, the Land of Cockaigne, and the source of military antagonism. It is not the individual contents of knowledge that matter, but the conformation of contents, and this was orientated to a specific warring fantasy. In this, the truth of individual statements is incidental.

The overriding need was to speak ill, and knowledge of Islam was a kind of defensive ignorance. Referring to Islam, Guibert de Nogent said in the twelfth century, "It is safe to speak evil of one whose malignity exceeds whatever ill can be spoken." Such evil as was and still is spoken in very tangible survivals of medievalism, is not purely arbitrary. It belongs to a repertoire of images and aesthetic judgements – judgements of value. Every culture thrives on establishing difference from others, and pursues this establishment of savage difference with particular energy in situations of serious external conflict or internal flux and uncertainty. It is often repeated that Jews in Europe were considered tokens of evil and scapegoats for issues with which they had no connection. Yet it is Islam and other orientals in this tokenist mode which have been most pervasively construed as an emblem of repellent otherness – it is not for nothing that Moses Hess, an early Zionist, took offence from the remark made by Bruno Bauer that the Jews were orientals.[3] For a person such as myself, whose vision of history is one of radical mutations, it is a strange matter indeed to observe such instances of an archetypal collective memory, of a dark area of cultural life alive with continuing folkloristic emblems – a study of recent Spanish clinical psychology, for instance, has revealed the pervasive and obsessive presence of the abominable Moor in Spanish fantasies.[4] This of course involves a process very commonly met with in psychological and ideological phenomena, the process of displacement, where one image stands for another to which it has a certain normative contiguity, or where one image or name is substituted for another with which it shares a certain property – in this case, unspeakable evil and horror. It is in this same emblematic mode that hysterical reactions are almost automatically triggered off today by such virtually interchangeable tokens of evil as communism, Shīʿīsm, Islam, terrorism, Arabism, Qadhafi, the PLO and a host of other phantasms nightly brought to our attention on television and in the other media, not to speak of fundamentalist Christians and media firebrands. Witness, for instance, the so-called prophecies of Nostradamus now in currency, where a dark apocalypse is constructed from Qadhafi, the Soviet Union and anti-Zionism.[5]

These persistent images are really less in direct continuity with the medieval image of the Saracen than mutant restatements of political and cultural antagonism. In the Middle Ages, they were born of the conflict between Islamic lands and Christendom – both before and after the Crusades, when Christendom became a unit of political thought, of geographical demarcation, and of cultural self-consciousness: the salient dates are the conquest of Sicily in 1060, the fall of Toledo in 1085 and the occupation of Jerusalem in 1099. Of this conflict were born the categories of Saracen and Moor. They, the observable instances of Islam, became the indices of a class of phenomena which are different, negative, fearsome. Orientalism, as a cultural mood and a component in a negative aesthetic repertoire, naturally had to be expressed in the prevailing literate cultural idiom of the times, and it is therefore not surprising that medieval orientalism represented Islam in terms of religious polemic, as religious idiom was the terrain where both antagonism and concord were encoded.

The Saracens thus were explained in terms of biblical legend as being of Hagarene descent, and Muhammad was thought of as a cardinal with frustrated papal ambitions; earlier, he had been thought of as one god among others worshipped by the Saracens; these included Mars, Plato, Apollo and what was termed Alkaron. In the plays and romances of the Middle Ages, Saracens came to be regarded as an index of repellent difference pure and simple. The term "Saracen" was applied indifferently to Muslims as to north European heathens, to Roman emperors, and to various disagreeable personalities in the Bible. William the Conqueror seems to have thought that he was engaged in battle with the Saracens of Britain.[6] It is not surprising, in the light of this general indexical function that shaped the categories of orientalism, that Muhammad should be endowed with sweeping evil universality. In Canto 28 of Dante's *Inferno*, he is relegated to the eighth of the nine circles of Hell, as a sower of schism and scandal, outdone in this by only Judas and Brutus.

Dante was a scholar; scholarship, in the Middle Ages as today, is inseparable from the cultural politics of its day, and knowledge never was, and will never be, an innocent endeavour, but was, and is, utterly sullied. Scholarship is the enunciation, in specialized terms for a specialized audience, of certain current principles which are, in scholarship, identified, concretized, categorized, ordered and concatenated. Medieval scholars of Islam conceived it as a form of Arianism; most notably, it was thought of in terms of biblical prophecy. Eulogius and Alvarus, not to speak of Nicetas, saw it as the preparation for the final appearance of the Antichrist, and such a view has been peculiarly resistant to time, change, rationality or progress. Duncan Black Macdonald, a jewel among orientalists, could still state in 1933 that Islam was a second-hand Arian heresy.[7] In 1597, an English Catholic exiled to the Continent spoke of Calvino-Turkism, in response to which the Anglican Matthew Sutcliffe spoke of Turko-Papism. Such attitudes had noble precedents. John Wycliffe had already seen Islam as the name for evil within the Church, and Luther himself, in a foreword to the 1543 edition of William of Ketton's Latin Koran, had declared that, whereas the pope was the head of the Antichrist, Islam was his body. Throughout the Reformation and well into the nineteenth century, Islam was seen as the lesser of the two horns of the ram made famous by the eighth chapter of the Book of Daniel, the greater horn being identified with the Pope. I myself witnessed such anti-Arab apocalyptic propaganda in Britain during the 1967 war. Hopeful crusading clerics even took heart from the appearance of Genghis Khan and his attack on Islamic domains; they saw in him a new David destined to fulfill the prophecies of Ezekiel.[8]

Let me remind you again that these conceptions existed among the learned public despite exact scholarship. In the shadow of the defeated Crusades, the Council of Vienne had, in 1312, ratified ideas previously canvassed by Roger Bacon and Raymond Lulle, which called for the learning of Arabic – this was in keeping with the times, as the receding Crusades were giving way to another way of carrying on the war, by missionary effort. These attitudes persisted despite the fact that chairs of Arabic were established in Paris and Oxford in 1539 and 1638; that the language was taught in Leiden from 1593; that the Arabic grammar of the Dutchman Erpenius and the dictionary of his student Golius, existed from the early seventeenth century.

We are not talking of two separate types and domains of knowledge about Islam, one for the scholarly elect and another for the rude masses, but of the coexistence within orientalism of two substantially concordant registers, one of which – the scholarly – has greater access to observation, as I have already indicated, and which looks all the more abject for this. Regardless of access to real or specious facts, facts are always constructed and their construction is invariably culture-specific. Orientalist scholarship is a cultural mood born of a mythological classificatory lore, a visceral, savage division of the world, much like such partisanship as animates support for football clubs. As in all myth and in primitive logic, difference gives way to antithesis in a play of binary structures. All cultures operate in terms of antithetical typologies of culture and savagery, of normalcy and disnature. It is in terms of these structures that Islam and things Islamic are construed, categorized, divided and connected, and it is such parameters that dictate the terms of discourse on things Islamic. It is quite inevitable that one's own culture is taken for the norm whose terms and whose language become the metalanguage of a cultural typology in which other cultures appear not merely as other, but as contrary. What happened during the long emergence of the bourgeois-capitalist order which Christendom became was that the evil which was Islam gradually became a want, a deficiency in the natural order of things which was this order itself seen, from the Enlightenment onwards, as the culmination of universal history. Islam, once evil vying with good, thus became an anachronism, a primitive stage in an emergent historicist notion of things.

This was certainly a derogation, and it was a derogation in terms of might. It was made possible by the actual superiority in terms of political, economic and technical power, which the bourgeois-capitalist order came to feel as a result of its universal expansion. Fear of the Saracen, of the Moor, of the Turk, once "the terrible scourge of the world", gave way to contempt, and the Ottoman Empire was soon to become the Sick Man of Europe. But it also gave way to enjoyment, which had become politically and culturally possible. Let me indicate, though, that European collective representations were not all nightmarish – a prurient fascination with things Islamic had titillated the libido of medieval monks no less than that of Lady Mary Montagu and of Alexander Pope.

Exoticism, frivolous or aesthetic admiration, is of course premised on an unreflected notion of utter otherness; it is a mode of consuming an object, of employing it for decorative and other purposes, in a context other than its own. Exoticism is a pleasant way of subjugating one's contrary, and ran closely parallel to the changing fortunes in the power relations between Europe and the domains of Islam. As early as 1454, at a banquet in Lille, a centrepiece of the entertainment was a tower carried on the back of an elephant lead by a gigantic Turk.[9] An art historian has spoken of the "oriental mode" in the work of Dürer, Bellini and others,[10] and indeed this persists today in illustrated editions of the Bible. Turkish and Persian carpets were in great vogue in the sixteenth and seventeenth centuries. Later, Charles II of England adopted Persian dress in court, in order to stop imitating French courtly costume. Samuel Pepys recorded that the new garment was quickly discarded as the king of France promptly ordered his footmen to be similarly dressed. There were more durable results of this exoticism, this containment and enjoyment of the bizarre; Islamist orientalism was to have a great artistic impact – I mention, at random, Marlowe's *Tamburlaine*, Goethe's *West-Östlicher Diwan*, Mozart's *Entführung aus dem Serail*, the art of Delacroix and Ingres, and the Brighton Pavilion. At close quarters, exoticism ceases to amuse and gives way to the barbarism that underpins it. Take for example the village of ʿAin Hud in occupied Palestine. It is a village for Israeli artists, and its title to special exotic privilege is one of characteristic grossness: it is the fact that its colourful houses in which the artists live have been left as they were when their owners and inhabitants were driven out in 1948.

Decorativeness is thus superimposed on subordination, one that is premised on eradicating the reality of the exotic. There is hardly anything Moorish about Othello but for the fatal magic handkerchief given to his mother by a witch, who was, incidentally, only Egyptian. Corneille criticized Racine for putting common Frenchmen in Turkish dress. This list can be extended at will. Otherness is always the context of deploying one's own concerns. Such was the admiration for Islam, however sullied and ambiguous, of, say, Condorcet, who considered it to be a natural religion in contradistinction to superstitious Christianity. Such is also the substance of artistic exoticism. For Dürer or Bellini, oriental themes and images were no more than visual frames for the depiction of biblical themes. The languid odalisques of Ingres are really derived from an antique sculpture, and they are given an oriental context and texture by motifs derived from the writings of Lady Mary Montagu and Montesquieu. Ingres had never been further south than Italy, and the same schematization in terms of genre and fancy is evident in nineteenth-century "ethnographic" painting of the Middle East.[11]

By the Enlightenment, therefore, Islam was no longer invariably and necessarily evil. It had also become something bizarre, distant, occasionally ridiculous. It had become a deficient order of things, and an order of deficient things. Deficiency is, of course, a polemical notion. It implies a requisite completeness, a consummate plenitude, in relation to which deficiency is measured. But this involves not only measurement: the correct order of things causes others to be seen and judged in its terms and on it own terms. The discourse involved is one of contrasts, very much like the primitive logic that underlay medieval and early modern conceptions. Alongside the continuing contrast of good with evil, orthodoxy with heresy, moral probity with libertinism and sodomy, the Enlightenment scheme of things required the presence of other players in this game, which it could call its own. These were reason, freedom and perfectibility, the three inclusive categories of the present epoch. Along with this, the birth of modern orientalist scholarship in the Enlightenment was accompanied by the secularization of the profession. Clerics gave way to traders, dilettantes, gentlemen of leisure, and to consuls. In the course of the nineteenth and twentieth centuries, journalists took the place of the dilettantes, salaried academics that of gentlemen of leisure, while colonialists and sundry spies joined the ranks of all categories. As scholarship always follows the flag, Napoleon's invasion of Egypt was accompanied by an army of scholars who produced the monumental *Description de l'Egypte*, and the French invasion by Algeria led to a prodigious scholarly effort. The *Journal Asiatique* was founded in 1823, the *Journal of the Royal Asiatic Society* in 1834, and the *Zeitschrift der deutschen morgenländichen Gesellschaft* in 1849.

The polemical structure of modern orientalist discourse is precisely premised on the definition of things Islamic in terms of contrasts of reason, freedom and perfectibility.[12] These yielded three major characteristics of things Islamic and from the topical clusters thus generated can be derived all the topics of orientalism and of Islamic studies, in an essential form complete and hardly altered since the mid nineteenth century. Those of you who are familiar with orientalist Islamic scholarship will readily recognize these topics. To reason corresponded enthusiastic unreason, politically translated as fanaticism, a major concern of nineteenth-century scholars and colonialists as of today's television commentators. This notion provided an explanation for political and social antagonism to colonial and post-colonial rule, by reducing political and social movements to motivations humans share with animals. Montesquieu, Hegel and many others saw Muslim politics as life in the whirlwind of fortune, an intensely sensuous life in which passion, that low manifestation of nature, reigns supreme. Such passion according to this paradigm has two outlets: fractious and predatory politics, or else vice. In both, we have an abstract enthusiasm. Energy in the secular world is geared towards negative purposes only and is incapable of setting up a mature political order. Thus politics of communities designated as Muslim are amorphous and infinitely pliable. Muslim cities are seen to be formless and fissiparous, and Muslim conquests and movements directionless and utterly wild. Muslim history is an absurd succession of events, time without duration, described by dynasties which Hegel said were "destitute of organic firmness", which belong "to mere space".[13] The corollary of this is a wretchedly dogmacentric life, a total abandonment of individuality to the exclusive worship of an abstract God. Another corollary to this, and the political analogue of this abject subjection of mind, will and person to God, is the subjection of individuality to collectivity, the oriental mirror image of freedom and its antithesis. From the eighteenth century, this topic was designated as oriental despotism, the irredeemable, immediate and unbridgeable gap between total tyrannical power on the one hand, and anarchy on the other. This theme,[14] developed by major thinkers like Montesquieu, has been applied by minor intellects to the study of Arabic and Islamic polities and political theory.

These two primary categories for the apprehension of things Islamic – unreason and servitude – posit Islam as a creature in diremption, as the unlikely coexistence of sheer animality on the one hand, and an abstract, hence forever forced and repressive, principle of order on the other. Nothing mediates the relation between the war of all against all on the one hand, and the Leviathan on the other; nothing mediates God and the world; one of them only is triumphant at a given moment. Civil society, the realm where individual needs are rationally co-ordinated, and that which brings forth the state, is unthinkable. It is little wonder that a variation of this theme has come increasingly to prominence. This is a characteristically dismal orientalist adaptation of the social sciences, one which views clan, tribe, locality, sect or ethnic group as a natural entity, one whose sole determinant is virtually a seminal pre-determination. It is at once a natural entity which refuses to be subdued by a higher principle of order such as the state, and a unit whose connection to its members is irrationally obligatory, and therefore despotic. Social groups, rather than being regarded as properly sociological categories, are looked upon as no more than involutions upon some infra-historical essence which does not admit of historical study except in the most banal sense, an infra-historical order which is ever present and which explains present-day events. These groups – sects, ethnic groups and other *dramatis personae* which populate orientalist discourse, which fill the pronouncements of experts and which come to us nightly on our television screens in stories of irrational carnage and outrage – such groups are seen as irreducibly specific, hence naturally antagonistic, endowed with a congenital propensity to factionalism. Thus communalism, which is a very recent phenomenon, is thought to be primordial. The title under which this animal existence is officiated is "identity", a hugely mystifying notion of great incidence and preference in expert opinion. It is this pathetic notion which is responsible for much of the nonsense one hears about the supposedly primordial antagonisms of Lebanon, about the conflict between Arabs and Berbers or between sedentary and tribal folk which animated French colonial historiography of North Africa.

The third category out of which things Islamic were identified and categorized is perfectibility. In the course of the nineteenth century this term, though not its meaning, fell out of use and was absorbed in the wider senses of evolutionism and historicism. And, indeed, the evolutionary schemata of world history, be they that of Condorcet, of Auguste Comte, of Hegel, Marx or Herbert Spencer, as of such theories as underlie development theory and the disastrous policies of the World Bank – all these theories can accommodate accounts of the specific differences which distinguish the oriental-Islamic from the occidental-normative. Normative and terminative correspond to one another in the evolutionist-historicist Eurocentric scheme: Islam, as anomaly, as a flaw, is seen to be an anachronism. Its characteristics – despotism, unreason, belief, stagnation, medievalism – belong to stages of history whose inferiority takes on a temporal dimension.

It is quite striking how the antithetical structures in terms of which Islam is apprehended run parallel to the manner in which feudalism has traditionally been regarded, and indeed the notion of primitivism shares many features with both the orient and feudalism. But over and above the explicit insertion of Islamic history within evolutionist schemes, such as the unusual position it occupies in Hegel's *Philosophy of History* or the peripheral position to which it is relegated in terms of the Asiatic mode of production, the historicity of Islam in terms of the philosophy of progress has been dubious. No properties of things Islamic were seen as contributory to the topical thematics of progress and evolution. Islamic history was and is still regarded as, at best, an accidental vehicle for the transmission of Greek learning to the West. As for its proper historicity, it is regarded in terms not of progress, but of decline; it is seen as an irrational irruption on to the canvas of history, an irruption which, for those of a generous disposition, carried a number of creditable principles. But it could only decline. Its original irrationality is implicitly seen in terms of either a doctrinal or a racial inadequacy. On assuming power, on founding a frenetically expanding empire, and sponging the wares of superior civilizations, this unworthy beginning can only realize its nemesis by very rapid corruption, senescence and atrophy. And this rapid fall is implicitly reducible to the discordance between the loftiness which some generous scholars ascribe to Islam's original impulse, and the dead weight of the Muslims' original irrationalism, their animal enthusiasm, the abstractness of their power, the formlessness of their societies. Whatever is construed as itself rational never goes beyond the bounds of the singular event to which it relates. Islamic history thus becomes, at best, a ponderous tragedy, at worst a soap opera, and in all cases a misadventure. Decline thus becomes not a fact of the historical order, but a predictable event of the metaphysical order. Decline is here not essentially a historical fact, but is natural given the antithetical conception of Islam employed: the antithesis of normalcy and nature is anomaly and disnature. Decline becomes metaphysically necessary, a foregone conclusion underlined by an actual disparity in might. That racist stereotypes and historical justification are concordant comes as no surprise.

Such are the schemata according to which modern orientalism conceives things Islamic. They should be recognizable to anyone studying the standard textbooks. They did not, and still do not, appear as simply the products of a collective imagination steeled with colonialism. On the contrary, they appeared, and still appear, as the result of direct observation and of scholarly endeavour. What gave them this prerogative was another result of the Enlightenment, and the backbone of Islamic studies: philology. Let us not forget how this philology grew, what fecund intellects worked for its establishment, and to what simplistic degradations it was subjected by orientalist Arabic philology. It was not only an outgrowth of antiquarian research; its beginnings were a rich web of antiquarian learning, and of criticism of the biblical text – Richard Simon's unconsummated work stands out, as does the more comprehensive albeit historically less influential work of Spinoza. Philological work on Sanskrit, and its later development into comparative Indo-European philology by Bopp are also crucial, as are the momentous later developments of biblical criticism and textual hermeneutics by the likes of Schleiermacher and (in a different direction) of Friedrich Strauss. The luxuriant writings of German Romantic historians, are also germane. In general, philology sought, with Spinoza, the separation between the sense of a text and its truth,[15] a truth which had been typologically or otherwise pre-given in traditional biblical exegesis. Philology rested in its decipherment of the world in the example of Vico, for instance, not on irreducible difference, but in similarity, hence accessibility to understanding on the basis of a humanity commonly shared by the philologist and by his charges.[16]

But altogether, orientalist philology in its Islamic-studies mode retained from this revolution in the historical sciences only two rudimentary elements. The first is the positivism of incipient philology – and I use "positivism" in the generic epistemological sense, without reference to evolutionist doctrine. Positivist philology was and is a discipline with a decidedly moralizing stance, a somewhat devotional sanctimoniousness, one which was described by one of the greatest classical philologists of the nineteenth century[17] in terms of asceticism and self-denial, which he contrasted with Nietzsche's *Birth of Tragedy*, a text which provoked the outburst I am referring to. Let us not forget that morality has no business in a world devoid of infamy, and that consequently the other side of this technicalist purity is technically accomplished fraud: in fact, the eighteenth and nineteenth centuries were the Golden Age of scientifically authenticated fraud. I need only remind you of Macpherson's Ossian, of Chatterton's medieval poetry and of the Chronicle of Richard of Cirencester. These textual contrivances are of the same type as taxidermy, also perfected in the nineteenth century, and both taxidermy and positivist philology aspire to an ideal of the same order.[18]

This pedantic aspect of positivist philology was not infrequently the object of ridicule; the original Larousse dictionary, for instance,[19] stressed this matter, but equally underlined the value of the discipline. This value resided, and still resides, in its pursuit of the sense of a text; it is a sort of ethnography of the past. In the field of Arabic, the tone was set by Antoine Isaac Sylvestre de Sacy, the father of Arabic philology in the West, who brought the full burden of his Jansenism to bear on his material. In his work as in that of his numerous students and of subsequent generations, somewhat critical editions of Arabic works have been established, lexica produced, the main factual outlines of Islamic history sketched in Western languages, the manuscript holdings of various European libraries inventorized – a process which was, incidentally, accompanied by the plunder of libraries in Muslim lands. Positivist philology aims for the "scientific" study of texts, of the meanings of their words and sentences, of the referents to which the text belongs: these are, according to a standard nineteenth-century textbook, historical facts, cultural life, religion, law and society.[20]

This exactitude of information and of designation which fired whatever spirit positivist philologists may have had, was animated by a typical Enlightenment motif, and was aimed at the seizure of the Real without the intervention of Passion. It is a form of vernacular realism. This realism does not yield the truth; it only yields discrete items of information, factoids, according to implicit criteria of selection which are fundamentally inhibitory, which work by a sort of censor principle not unlike that of the naturalistic novel.[21] Naturalism is fundamentally a censor, a defence against passion, and positivist realism is essentially antiseptic. In the field of philology it is the scholarly counterpart of bureaucratic rationality. It produces a disorganized array of these factoids according to a rudimentary principle of positivist epistemology, that the linguistic sign and the real signified can be made directly to correspond without any mediation – this view is contradicted, of course, by linguistic science, by cognitive psychology and by the history of art. Semantics thus gives way to an abstract lexicalism, and the unfounded supposition is made that the meanings of words, of terms, of beliefs, of doctrines, no less than of dogmas, of texts and of statements, are univocal and can therefore be uncovered once their origin has been exposed. The cardinal principle in the face of which positivist philology flies is an ancient principle of rhetoric, now brought back to prominence by linguistics and discourse analysis; namely, that all things involving words have to deal with the technical problems of words. And the key to these is neither the lexicon nor the grammatical compendium, but the properties and rules of semantics, the structure of text, the construction of discourse, the infinite resources of language, the rhetoric of meaning and reality, the boundless ambiguity of the text. No text has an intrinsic and univocal objectivity of meaning; it is always context-specific, internally and externally, and thus open only to structural analyses.

What positivism thus seeks to establish is not scientific knowledge, but naturalistic apprehension. Its entire project is based on the notion of verisimilitude which is ultimately a visual metaphor, and vision is, of course, the most primitive of cognitive means. Knowledge is modelled on a sensuous paradigm of immediacy, as a mimetic rendition of "reality" full of the concreteness of immediate life. Such a project in fact is far from a consummated naturalism, and is closer to the Romantic notion of poetry, albeit unspeakably inferior to it.

Thus positivist philology is a genetic mode of study, an indication by a term of its origin. I do not call it historical because it lacks the totalizing orientation of modern historical scholarship. It seeks to describe past events – words, occurrences, dogmas, or whatever – according to the famous but unremarkable and not very profound aphorism of Leopold van Ranke, that he wrote history "wie es eigentlich gewesen", a teasing phrase which, with or without justification, has come to embody the historiographical utopia of the nineteenth century. This genetic investigation seeks the explanation of things in terms of their origins, and produces inventories of correspondence which are then served up as causal chains: texts fragmented and their parts reduced to other texts, events explained by single antecedents, fragments of dogmas explained by scriptural fragments, totally without respect to the fact that, even if, let us say, dogmas are explicitly set out in terms of scriptures, this does not mean they are derived from them except in the banal sense that a scripture, like any other text, is almost infinitely interpretable, and universally deferred to. The true meaning of a text, by contrast, is historical; a text has no sense outside the various and contradictory traditions that appropriate it. Even fundamentalists invoke the original text to the exclusion of commentary in order to substitute their own novel glosses. No end is really prefigured in its beginning. The resulting picture is of scholarship which is almost entirely enumerative, enumerating instances of an origin and variations therefrom, a very extreme form of philosophical realism totally oblivious to the fact that, even if it were possible to identify origins – and this is a very dubious proposition – it is surely impossible to make an exhaustive inventory of beginnings and thus arrive at an approximation of the Truth, genetically conceived, of course. The event and the explanation of the event are therefore of the same order: the order of narrative is at the same time the order of explanation and comprehension; vision and reason are united in a poetic reverie in the guise of an exacting philological severity.

Thus orientalist scholarship piles fact upon fact and date upon date in an order ostensibly blind to all but real succession. But this research is always geared towards the discovery of origin. It is not at all surprising that the overwhelming volume of orientalist research into Islamic matters has investigated beginnings, historical beginnings and Koranic textual beginnings. It has claimed to find in these beginnings the fount, origin and explanation of the whole sad story of Islamic history, institutions, societies and thought. From the Koran this scholarship has derived the principles of economic life and the supposed failure of capitalism. From the same text it seeks to explain the actual source of history. From the principle of *jihād*, holy war, one of the most eminent orientalists in Britain today derived all political activity in India, Turkey, the Levant, Iran, Spain and the Sudan over 1,200 years.[22] From the conflict of ʿAlī and Muʿāwiya, orientalist scholarship seeks to explain the war between Iran and Iraq. If you looked at the "explanations" of the Iranian revolution and of the Iran–Iraq war, you would find yourselves in the company of much discussion of the so-called "martyrdom complex" of Shīʿīsm, of the death, nearly 1,400 years ago, of Husain. You will find hardly any discussion of Iranian history over the past hundred years or so. Islamic studies is thus a cluster of pseudo-causal chains. These chains are meant eventually to be reducible to the irreducible essence of Islam, which really performs an explanatory function very much akin to that of Phlogiston in eighteenth-century chemistry. The result is that elusive origins are sought, and the actual course, outcome, institutions and processes of Islamic history and culture are ignored, except under the metaphysical auspices of the study of "decline".

This is of course a retrospective construction, a casting of the origin in the light of subsequent events, which flies in the face of the most elementary principles of historical scholarship. Scholars working in this field have always sanctimoniously claimed "objectivity"; yet their procedure is imbued with a vast meta-historical principle, an origin of origins, the pseudo-cause of other pseudo-causes, which is presupposed in Islamic studies. An irreducible substance is posited, one to which all occurrences in Islamic history are reducible – other occurrences are decreed anomalous and of non-Islamic origin. What we witness is not a genuinely barren agnosticism, in which many orientalists take pride, except seldom; what we find is not literally a display of what Croce called the "sumptuous ignorance" of philological history, nor simply what Lord Acton praised as "colourless" writing. What are at play in the naturalism of Islamic studies, in the censor principle mentioned, are enunciations which are not formless, nor simply polemical and directed outwards, nor again devoid of passion. Islamist discourse is thoroughly and irredeemably structured by implicit ideological notions, notions which identify things as Islamic, as original, and which organize the world of things Islamic in terms of the European imagination, and of the colonialist and neo-colonialist management of the world. It is not only that the unreflected and uncritical assortment of factoids must be the victim of implicit ideologies, folkloristic images and racist stereotypes. These facts have to be identified as relevant, others have to be rejected as irrelevant, sequences of putative influence have to be judged as plausible, others are unthinkable, all in the name of the naturalistic mode.

History is thus captive to meta-historical schemata; it is structured by a poetics, according to the terms of Hegel's analysis of history, epic and poetry in the third book of his *Aesthetics*. It is structured by the three meta-historical notions I spoke of: unreason, despotism and backwardness. Each is in fact a class of topics, of criteria of selection and of relevance, and together they set the boundaries of that which is thinkable. It is assumed that there are a number of intrinsic substantive qualities which characterized a changeless, or only superficially changeable *homo islamicus*: a creature born of distance, not only of the antithetical distance I have spoken of, but of the accompanying political distance established by colonialism.

I have already spoken about the character of this *homo islamicus*, of how he is defined by the inversion of the three cardinal notions through which the bourgeois-capitalist epoch conceives itself:

reason, freedom and perfectibility. To this schematization of the self corresponds the schematism of the other. Each of these schemata is a topic which is invariably called forth to schematize things that are observed Islamic. Thus there are "Islamic cities" unlike all other cities, "Islamic economies" to which economic reason is inapplicable, "Islamic polities" impenetrable to social sciences and political sense, "Islamic history" to which the normal equipment of historical research is not applied. Facts are disassociated from their historical, social, cultural and other contexts, and reduced to this substantive Islamism of the European imagination. Accurate detail becomes local colour, a mere enhancement of naturalism, a "reality-effect".[23] This is why orientalism in its Islamist mode is a mode of perception and apprehension, not of knowledge. It identifies things as Islamic, and does not know them as historical. It names things as Islamic, and at the same stroke endows them with the changeless and ageless characteristics of the *homo islamicus*. This is another reason why Islamic studies is, as I have already said, exhaustively enumerative: the identification of things as Islamic by their reduction to a textual Islamic origin is what it considers to be its proper task. Things Islamic, when identified with a beginning, add nothing to their origin. They have no specificity defined in terms of their historical circumstances and apart from the meta-historical specificity of their origin. This accounts, incidentally, for the dull repetitiveness which many scholars believe they see in Islamic history; it accounts even more so for the implicit uneventfulness and lack of real change in which is premised this genetic study, this degraded form of historicism. All in all, things Islamic are uniform, indistinct, isomorphous. This is of course a thoroughly unhistorical view. Revolutionary Iran is as far from Saudi Arabia as tenth-century Islam in Spain is distinct from contemporary Iran. One needs to substitute "Christianity" for "Islam" to see how ridiculous the picture will look. It is true that Bantu messianism and revolutionary Nicaraguan Jesuitism are both Christian. But this is a far cry from assuming their essential identity, or from assuming their indistinctness except in appearance from say, atavistic Catholicism in Poland or the politics of the Reverend Ian Paisley, or, for that matter, from Maronitist politics in Lebanon. Anyone who asserts the essential identity of Cathars, Flagellants, Rasputin and the Dutch Reformed Church will surely be pronounced mad. European scholars of Islam are in a strange league with Muslim fundamentalism. Both espouse a savage essentialism, a changeless ahistorical irreducibility, a mythical "real" Islam independent of time and existent only at the beginning of things Islamic and at its pristine fount. Both insist that a rigourist form of religiosity is the characteristic, the real, of which Islam in places as different as twentieth-century Turkey and tenth-century Canton are mere avatars, any difference between these two Islams, or between aspects of them and the supposed pristine condition, is relegated to mere incidentals. Both fundamentalism and orientalism therefore eliminate the major part of history: rigourist fundamentalism was only very seldom espoused, and always by very small minorities, and the historical reality of Islam, as of other religions, is the normal course of events in which fundamentalist moments are incidental. One cannot use the brand of Christianity propagated by the Reverend Jerry Falwell as an explanatory principle with which to unravel the reality of Philip II's Most Catholic dominions. Fundamentalists realize the wildest fantasies of orientalism; for the former, as for the latter, the striving is for a myth of origin.

Yet the Islamism of things Islamic is only convincing because it is a classificatory token upon which scholarship is superimposed, a token of political and cultural otherness. In this otherness, things are levelled for ideological convenience. Things Islamic therefore duplicate each other. Studies have shown[24] how this takes place, how the structures of society duplicate those of theology, how theology structurally duplicates the essential features of despotic devotions, how these themselves duplicate the structures of power and of morality, how the whole of history is deployed to show the changeless integrity of the *homo islamicus*. Orientalist discourse on Islam indeed presents it through "a set of representative figures",[25] a vocabulary and a repertoire of plastic images which are invariably encountered – much like the repertoire of plots, textual units and their permutations which account for the repetitiveness of science fiction, folk tales and pornography. All that cannot be made liable to reduction to these topics and notions of orientalist Islam is denied to Islam: thus Arab–Islamic philosophy is seen as only nominally so; Sufism, spiritually rich, is forced into the modes of heresy and non-Islamic provenance; the celebrated Ibn Khaldūn was made into a precursor of positivism and other European doctrines, or, in extreme cases, a representative of the Berbero-European anti-Arab spirit, all by virtue of his supposed modernity.[26] Indeed, virtually the whole of Muslim intellectual history is written in terms of a supposed conflict between Reason and Belief, the one foreign and the other native. This is not really very different from certain medieval processes of thought: some of you might know that medieval writers, in awe of and in admiration for Saladin, explained his excellence by asserting that his mother was one Countess of Pontieu.

In effect, the orientalist rendition of Islam is only putatively historical. The rejection by traditional orientalist scholarship, as by nineteenth-century historical and philological scholarship, of what it termed "speculation" is really the counterpart of this. It was only natural that emergent disciplines should distance themselves from others; the nineteenth century saw the professionalization of history, and the attempt to suppress its rhetorical status. Chairs of history were established in Berlin in 1810 and in Paris in 1812, but in Britain it was only in 1866 that a chair of history was established at Oxford. Great historians like Guizot and Michelet were dismissed for teaching "ideas" rather than facts. But one can clearly see that the rejection of positivism, idealism and Romanticism in nineteenth-century historiography and orientalist philology was nominal and institutional, not conceptual. Orientalist philology, as I have tried to show, is nothing but thoroughly structured by positivist epistemology and an essential category of Islam. Instead of the antiquarianist ideal, the result of this is the enemy of antiquarianism, what is derisively termed *histoire romanesque.*

Thus in the orientalist study of Islam are aborted both the full possibilities of positivism and of historical study. The possibilities of positivism are aborted because the field of relevant facts is severely circumscribed, and the facts themselves severely schematized. The possibilities of historical study are aborted because of the genuinely ahistorical character of the genetic reductionism I have spoken of. Historicism is used antithetically; it does not seek to look for genuine changes and transformations, to chart the course of history, but to fix distance, to affirm the Islamism of Islamic history, that is, to reduce it to its schematized meta-historical components, which affirm the antithetical difference of things Islamic from things normal. This is why orientalist Islamic studies have been so peculiarly resistant to the acquisitions and advances of the modern historical, including the social, sciences and to the normal procedures of philological and historical study today. This is also why many of my fellow-professionals in this field work on history in total oblivion of historical methodology, or literature in total innocence of critical theory (or even any inclination to literature), on grammar with hardly any awareness of linguistics. This is so much the case that there is hardly any perceptible change in the essential categorical, thematic and conceptual baggage of Islamic studies in more than a century; works supersede one another only by the addition of detail. But the features I have outlined, and the profound anti-intellectualism which animates the profession of Islamic studies, are essential for the survival of Islam as a category of orientalist discourse. The profession lumbers on with the disquieting confidence of its anti-intellectualism. It is still not unusual to take such library skills as are requisite in the editing of manuscripts and the collating of sources to be adequate indications of consummate scholarship. It is equally common in view of this involuted cultural homeliness to regard some form of contact with Muslim countries to be adequate for intellectual mastery of the area, and thus to hold "experience" as an adequate substitute for study and lived exposure to "Islam" as perfect substitutes for scholarship.

Not at all unlike sympathetic magic, contagion is seen as the cause of effectiveness, and partial contiguity in space is taken for mastery of the whole. Again not unlike magic, this is a technique of control. Expertise in Islamic or Middle Eastern matters is thus unrelated to learning; learning is one thing, and expertise is quite another matter, connected less with knowledge than with belonging to particular circles which politicians and businessmen endow with oracular qualities, less because of reliability than because of a unity of practical purpose – diplomacy, war, subversion and profit, with the occasional tinge of romanticism. The context of practical expertise in which studies of Islam and of the Middle East find themselves is premised on the protean quality of Islam I have spoken of, and can only be preserved with the systematic resistance of the discipline to the present conditions and requirements of historical and sociological scholarship. The Islam of Islamic studies is not "out there", but is a politico-cultural canon. Without it, many people would find themselves out of a job.

Thus, abandoned to the native intelligence, to folkloristic images, to a spurious notion of objectivity, the very premises of Islamic studies are radically and thoroughly unsound; their very foundation, the identification and the construal of relevant facts, is based upon a political and cultural imagination. This corresponds to what has been called the "intoxicating Orient of the mind", a "state between dreaming and walking where there is no logic ... to keep the elements of our memory from attracting each other into their natural combinations".[27] Thus the only possible attitude for historical scholarship towards the entire tradition of European Islamic studies is one of a very radical scepticism. One may be prepared to accept some bibliographical and textual-critical results of this tradition. But any proper writing of Islamic history has to rest on the dissolution of Islam as an orientalist category. It will have to start with putting into question the very notion of objectivity itself – or rather, to regard it as a historical category and as a historical and discursive problem. It will have to come to terms with the prodigious intellectual revolution inaugurated by Marx. It will have to take account of the fact that narrative, born out of fiction, myth and epic,[28] is on the wane in the study of history, and that not reality but intelligibility is the cornerstone of modern historical scholarship. It will have to take full account of the discovery of historical discontinuity and bear out the full consequences thereof, as of the rejection of "origin".[29] Full account has, moreover, to be taken of modern philology and rhetoric, and the simplifications of notions such as "influence",[30] and gear itself towards "fields of sense" and associated categories[31] and towards the acquisitions of modern critical theory as in the work of Benjamin, Frye, Barthes and others and the theory of discursive formations. It has to liberate itself from Islam, and scrutinize Islamic histories, societies, economies, temporalities, cultures and sciences with the aid of history, of economics, of sociology, critical theory and anthropology. Only then will Islam be disassociated, and reconstituted as historical categories amenable to historical study. In this, positivist philological research is axial. But this is only in the sense that it is to be presupposed; like literacy, it is the elementary beginning, not the end of research and study.

Notes

1. In what follows I have drawn on the following: J. Fück, *Die arabischen Studien in Europa*, Leipzig 1955; N. Daniel, *Islam and the West*, Edinburgh 1960; R.W. Southern, *Western Views of Islam in the Middle Ages*, Cambridge, MA 1962; J. Kritzeck, *Peter the Venerable and Islam*, Princeton 1964; N. Daniel, *Islam, Europe, and Empire*, Edinburgh 1966; A.-T. Khoury, *Polémique byzantine contre l'Islam (VIII–XIIIe)*, Leiden 1972; D. Metlitzki, *The Matter of Araby in Medieval England*, New Haven

and London 1977; B.P. Smith, *Islam in English Literature*, 2nd edn, New York 1977; E.W. Said, *Orientalism*, London 1978; E.W. Said, *Covering Islam*, London 1981; A. Abdel-Malek, "L'Orientalisme en crise", *Diogène*, 44, 1963, pp. 109–42; M. Rodinson, "The Western Image and Western Studies of Islam", in J. Schacht and E. Bosworth, eds, *The Legacy of Islam*, Oxford 1974, pp. 9–62; A. Laroui, "The Arabs and Cultural Anthropology: Notes on the Method of Gustave von Grunebaum", in *The Crisis of the Arab Intellectual*, Berkeley and Los Angeles 1976, pp. 44–80; ʿA. Al-ʿAẓma, "Ifṣāḥ al-istishrāq", *Al-Mustaqbal al-ʿArabi*, 4/32, 1981, pp. 43–62 and the shortened version published as A. Al-Azmeh, "The Articulation of Orientalism", *Arab Studies Quarterly*, 3, 1981, pp. 384–402.

2. *A True and Faithful Account*, preface, pp. 13, 18, 21. On printers' requirements, see Daniel, *Islam, Europe and Empire*, p. 14.

3. J. Carlebach, *Karl Marx and the Radical Critique of Judaism*, London 1978, p. 140.

4. T.F. Glick, *Islamic and Christian Spain in the Early Middle Ages*, Princeton 1979, pp. 3, 317 n. 1.

5. J.-C. de Fontbrune, *Nosterdamus. Historien et prophète*, Paris 1981, pp. 352ff, 381ff.

6. Metlitzki, *The Matter of Araby*, p. 119.

7. D.B. Macdonald, "Whither Islam?", *Muslim World*, 23, 1933, p. 2.

8. M. Eliade, *The Myth of Eternal Return*, transl. W.R. Trask, London 1955, p. 142.

9. J. Huizinga, *The Waning of the Middle Ages*, transl. F. Hopman, Harmondsworth 1972, p. 241.

10. J. Raby, *Venice, Dürer and the Oriental Mode (Hans Huth Memorial Studies, 1)*, London 1982.

11. M. Steven, "Western Art and its Encounter with the Islamic World, 1798–1914", in M.A. Stevens, ed., *The Orientalists: Dalacroix to Matisse*, London 1984, pp. 17, 21.

12. Al-ʿAẓma, "Ifṣāḥ al-istishrāq".

13. G.W.F. Hegel, *The Philosophy of History*, transl. J. Sibtree, New York 1956, p. 105.

14. For the despotism theme, see A. Grosrichard, *Structure du sérail. La fiction du déspotisme asiatique dan l'Occident classique*, Paris 1979; and the observations on Montesquieu by L. Althusser, *Politics and History*, transl. B. Brewster, London 1972, pp. 75ff.

15. T. Todorov, *Symbolisme et interpretation*, Paris 1978, pp. 128ff.

16. E. Auerbach, 'Giambattista Vico and die Idee der Philologie', in *Hometange a Antonio Rubio i Lluch*, Barcelona 1936, vol. 1, pp. 293–304.

17. U. von Wilamowitz-Möllendorf, *Zukunftsphilologie. Eine Erwiderung auf Friedrich Nietzsches "Geburt des Tragödie"*, Berlin 1872, p. 32.

18. See the discussion of S. Bann, *The Clothing of Clio*, Cambridge 1984, pp. 16ff.

19. Paris 1866, vol. 12, p. 823, col. 4.

20. A. Gercke and E. Norden, eds, *Einleitung in die Altertumswissen-*

schaften, Berlin and Leipzig 1910–12, vol. 1, pp. 35–6.

21. N. Frye, *The Anatomy of Criticism*, Princeton 1971, pp. 51–2.

22. Said, *Covering Islam*, p. 108.

23. R. Barthes, "L'Effet du réel", *Communications*, 11, 1968, pp. 84–9.

24. See ʿAẓma, "Ifṣāḥ al-Istishrāq"; and Laroui, "The Arabs and Cultural Anthology".

25. Said, *Orientalism*, p. 71.

26. See A. Al-Azmeh, *Ibn Khaldūn in Modern Scholarship*, London 1981.

27. P. Valéry, "Orientem Versus", in P. Valéry, *History and Politics*, transl. D. Folliot and J. Mathews, New York 1962, p. 381.

28. R. Barthes, "Historical Discourse", in *Structuralism. A Reader*, ed. M. Lane, London 1970, p. 155.

29. M. Foucault, *The Archaeology of Knowledge*, transl. A.M. Sheridan Smith, London 1972, pp. 3ff, 141ff.

30. For a statement of classical philology, see E. Auerbach, *Introduction aux études de philologie romane*, Frankfurt 1949, p. 27.

31. For instance, J. Trier, *Des Deutsche Wortschatz im Sinnbezirk des Verstandes*, Heidelberg 1931; and P. Ricoeur, *The Rule of Metaphor*, transl. R. Czerny et al., London 1978, p. 103.

32. G. Dumézil, *L'Héritage indo-européen à Rome*, Paris 1949, pp. 34–6, 42.

Index